DATA GAME

DATA GAME
The Story of Liverpool FC's
ANALYTICS REVOLUTION

JOSH WILLIAMS

First published by Pitch Publishing, 2024
Reprinted 2024
2

Pitch Publishing
9 Donnington Park,
85 Birdham Road,
Chichester,
West Sussex,
PO20 7AJ
www.pitchpublishing.co.uk
info@pitchpublishing.co.uk

© 2024, Josh Williams

Every effort has been made to trace the copyright. Any oversight will be rectified in future editions at the earliest opportunity by the publisher.

All rights reserved. No part of this book may be reproduced, sold or utilised in any form or transmitted in any form or by any means, electronic or mechanical, including photocopying, recording or by any information storage and retrieval system, without prior permission in writing from the Publisher.

A CIP catalogue record is available for this book from the British Library.

ISBN 978 1 80150 693 9

Typesetting and origination by Pitch Publishing
Printed and bound by Short Run Press Ltd, Exeter

Contents

Author's Note 7

1. Learning How to Count. 13
2. The Big Bang 25
3. Cowboys 43
4. 1,102 Ways to Get Worse 55
5. The Art of Dying 71
6. The Goldilocks Zone 93
7. Jürgen 105
8. Einstein 116
9. Truth Serum 129
10. Transformers 144
11. Pitch Control 158
12. Playing Chess with Loaded Dice 171
13. A Different Type of Arms Race 185
14. The Rise of the Machines 202
15. Liverpool 2.0 218

Works Cited 230

Author's Note

I'VE ALWAYS loved football. I've been obsessed with my favourite sport for as long as I can remember, and like many of you who are reading this book, my earliest memory is probably attempting to score as many goals as possible on the school yard. We've all done it. The person who owned the ball decided who could and couldn't play in the game, and if you were wearing a coat you knew it was about to be transformed into a makeshift goalpost. Before kick-off, the really important details got decided. 'I'm Michael Owen,' said one of my friends. 'I'm Robbie Fowler,' said another. I always used to enter the argument from a different place, armed with as much knowledge as possible from Championship Manager, the popular video game known as Football Manager today. 'I'm Anthony Le Tallec,' I would shout, knowing all about Liverpool's newest wonderkid acquisition from Le Havre. Martín Palermo from Boca Juniors was another favourite of mine, as was Ronaldinho, who played for Grêmio at the time, and Andrés D'Alessandro of River Plate.

As a child growing up on Merseyside who didn't have access to much live football on television, I was introduced to Championship Manager before the latest version of

FIFA. My cousin, Dom, who's 11 years older than me, used to manage one team, and I'd manage a rival in the same division. He lived in the same house as my dad, so I'd see him every Sunday without fail and we'd spend hours making progress on our save. Before I even knew how to swim or ride a bike, I was getting to grips with a tactics board on the most oversized desktop computer that you can imagine, instructing Roberto Carlos to advance towards the final third by drawing an arrow out of his position on the left side of the pitch. I managed Real Madrid often, for obvious reasons. Dom used to choose Valencia. He wanted more of a challenge.

I've always wondered whether that curious initiation had a subtle impact on how I ended up viewing the game. I remember writing numbers that I couldn't even pronounce on pieces of paper during lessons in school, with those supposed to represent transfer fees. I would place bids for my friends as some sort of infantile sporting director, knowing who was worth the most after playing alongside them on the yard. This is how I viewed the world of football as a young Scouser who still relied on the nearest adult to tie his shoelaces. Around 15 years later, I was still playing Football Manager, albeit without the threat of being outshone by a sibling in charge of a competitor. My tactical understanding of the sport had developed a little by that stage, so I decided to create a Twitter account as a means of documenting my virtual management, while also sharing my strategic thoughts on real-life matches.

Jürgen Klopp was one of the coolest coaches in the world at the time, with his intense and relentless brand of offensive football at Borussia Dortmund making headlines in England. 'I know it's not the most important statistic, but I love when I read after the game that we ran more than the opponent,' said the German in a famous interview with Sky Sports. Given the nature of the Premier League, it didn't take long before distance covered became the divine metric for broadcasters to highlight during live matches. It was the latest trend, and running more was suddenly all that mattered, resulting in the birth of my username, @ DistanceCovered, which has remained attached to me as some form of alias ever since.

My original plan was to write about my tactical approach to Football Manager, but I fancied a shot at writing about real-life football after a few months. Looking back at my first effort, it wasn't too bad. I decided to write about the summer business that Manchester City should conduct, having recently hired Pep Guardiola. Ederson was one of my suggestions based on his time at Benfica, and I also recommended AS Monaco's Fabinho, who later signed for Liverpool, and a young Alex Grimaldo.

Around 18 months after my beginning as a small-time analyst who had no real plan for his future and still worked in a supermarket, a job role emerged at Reach. The company, which owned the likes of the *Mirror, Liverpool Echo* and *Manchester Evening News* hoped to land the services of a writer who essentially had the knowledge of a scout. The successful candidate would be expected to analyse matches, players, managers and transfers in great detail, using evidence rather than clichés to deconstruct mainstream talking points. I remember almost tearing up as I headed to my interview in London, not because I was scared or worried, but because this was my ticket out of the supermarket. This was my chance to earn a living by doing what I had been doing since I was a toddler, or at least that was how I felt. In truth, I probably wasn't ready to represent one of the UK's biggest newspaper groups, and I certainly wasn't officially qualified. All my qualifications lay in the work that I had done for free over the course of the previous year, paying for my own personal Wyscout subscription and regularly tweeting my thoughts on the beautiful game for anybody who cared. I did have a degree in business, but my passion was football. Luckily for me, a diamond by the name of Jon Birchall decided I was worth taking a chance on.

When I made my start at Reach about a month later, I was struck by the demand for content. An emphasis was placed on volume, and that's perhaps an understatement, which made things difficult considering I held an interest in diving deep into ideas before carefully concluding my thoughts. I was expected to produce a minimum of three articles per day – which felt like a lot at the time – and I wasn't in control of the exaggerated headlines attached to my work. Editors from up and down the country would send specific requests to my line manager, who would then feed them to me. I distinctly remember being asked to write about Lincoln City at one stage, knowing that I had never watched them play a single minute of football. I had no choice but to adapt, because I simply didn't have enough spare time to deconstruct the inner workings of the Imps using video footage alone, so I started to incorporate numbers into my work.

Maths wasn't my strongest subject at school. I failed at GCSE level, in fact, but I very quickly started to realise that by consulting the underlying data attached to performances, you could gain a pretty accurate gauge of what was happening under the hood, as long as you could add the context that was lacking. I originally applied numbers to articles as a shortcut of sorts, but they gradually managed to convince me of their wisdom. By having a quick glance at the data and filtering out the noise, I felt I was able to paint quite an accurate picture of any team's fortunes, often without having to watch a second of footage.

Ever since, my belief that football can be quantified, at least to some extent, has gone from strength to strength. As I started to get to grips with life at Reach while improving my interpretation of the numbers, I recognised that Liverpool were consistently getting things right in the transfer market. With the man behind the rise of the almighty distance covered metric now occupying the Anfield hot seat, the Reds were steadily evolving with every passing window. I had witnessed Liverpool sign the likes of Paul Konchesky, Christian Poulsen, Josemi, Jan Kromkamp and David N'Gog over the years, but something had changed. The hit rate had dramatically improved almost overnight, and although Klopp deserved most the credit as the club's messiah, his genius was clearly being reinforced by Liverpool's brain behind the scenes, consisting of a team of experts who were tasked with installing Fenway Sports Group's vision for the Reds to become a scientific institution, just like the Boston Red Sox in the world of baseball. Liverpool suddenly seemed to master the art of squad building that had consumed my interest dating back to my childhood in charge of Madrid.

I've attended multiple conferences during my time as a writer, listening to trailblazing scientists such as Ian Graham and Will Spearman explain their efforts to solve football as part of a pioneering data science department on Merseyside. Liverpool's secrets have almost been drip-fed into the public domain over the past few years, and given my role at Reach, my Football Manager background and my natural curiosity as a supporter of the club, I've tried to piece the puzzle together.

The narrative associated with how the Reds became champions of everything under Klopp tends to follow a specific path, but I like to think this book represents a bit of an alternative story to the one that will be passed through the generations. This book is my attempt to credit those who perhaps drifted under the radar during Liverpool's rise. It's a ten-year tale, and one that challenges some of the accounts of what actually happened during the club's emotional journey to the pinnacle of the sport, with a specific focus on how data and tactics shaped Liverpool's future. I hope you enjoy reading it as much as I enjoyed writing it. Whether you're an avid follower of my work or you're coming across my name for the very first time, thank you for being a part of this project.

Chapter One

Learning How to Count

YOU'LL FIND a wide variety of different people in Las Vegas, Nevada. The first-timers, the newly-weds, the selfie-obsessed tourists, the high-rollers, the alcoholics, the locals who have seen it all, and the professional gamblers. John Henry assumed the form of the latter in 1971, or at least that was his intention. The subdued and reserved American, who had only been legally allowed to gamble for a little over 12 months, had parked himself at a blackjack table in one of the city's many casinos in an attempt to win big by minimising the element of chance through the application of mathematics. For most of the players surrounding him, winning was determined by little more than fate, hope and good fortune. It's in the lap of the gods, many amateur punters would suggest. Betting was about chance, destiny and randomness for the man on the street. For Henry, winning was determined by more than that, it was about probability. It was about gaining even the smallest upper hand.

He had developed a natural feel for numbers throughout his childhood years. Henry was a maths whizz in school, and as he was growing up, he was learning about how to use his numerical skills to navigate the practical realities of life. He wasn't in Vegas for a good time, attending shows and visiting tourist attractions wasn't on his to-do list. The trip was all business, albeit before he'd truly entered that world. Henry was attempting to acquire a marginal edge through the strategy of card counting. In simple terms, keeping track of what cards have been dealt, and using that information to evaluate whether the dealer has an advantage or not. He would later produce a paper on the concept alongside one of his instructors at the University of California, but before he was able to beat the odds and strike it rich, a voice politely asked him to leave the premises. While card counting without any outside aid isn't technically illegal in Vegas, casinos do tend to reserve the right to tactfully remove those who are suspected of counting. 'I can count multiple decks,' Henry said. 'It's not hard.'

A farmer from a young age, Henry was destined for a different path to his ancestors. He inherited his family's 1,000-acre soybean farm after his father's death – which happened a few years after his trip to Vegas – but rather than continuing past traditions by planting, growing and harvesting corn, cotton and rice, Henry broke the mould by predicting the futures of his products. 'Most farmers want to talk about their tractors,' said a local friend who managed his own nearby farm, 'but all John wanted to talk about was the market and prices.' The man who would later own Liverpool Football Club as the face of a multinational consortium made his fortune as a commodities trader before exploring sports. 'If you follow your bliss, you put yourself on a kind of track that has been there all the while, waiting for you,' he said in an interview with ESPN. 'That's what led me into the financial world, because I enjoyed applying mathematics to markets, and it was a profound challenge that resonated within me.'

Trading could be quite intimidating for newcomers, even the smartest and most prepared operators. The stock exchange was prone to descending into utter chaos as floor traders fought to get ahead, and that anarchy epitomised the nature of the market. Bright colours and numbers indicating price changes would battle for the spotlight in every direction, with people yelling, shouting and waving papers, almost as though they were trying to place a last-minute bet on a horse race. Beginners usually followed one of two paths upon testing the turbulent waters of the investment world. Some would react with horror before searching for the nearest exit door, whereas others reacted with intrigue, appreciating the lack of sense in front of them before wanting to delve deeper in search of logic. Henry sided with the latter, recognising the many inefficiencies attached to his early experiences toying with stocks and shares. He has been described as having a 'laser-like focus' by Mark Rzepczynski, who was president of Henry's investment firm for nine years between 1998 and 2007. That was outlined as his big secret to success. 'If he was looking at a table or chart of numbers, he could look at pages and pages and find the one wrong number,' said Rzepczynski.

A college dropout, Henry's trade investments were guided by data, which was an approach designed to remove bias, ego and emotion from the decision-making process.

He was entirely dispassionate as an investor, and created his own sophisticated algorithm at the start of his journey by gathering historical price data from public libraries and using a hand calculator to challenge the accuracy of his models. Technological limitations curbed the wisdom of his work, but his methods were still far more progressive than most of his fellow investors. It was a pioneering approach at the time that integrated a degree of intellect and process into an otherwise hectic and almost senseless exercise. Back then, the average trader was ruled by gut feelings. It was a lottery, it was glorified gambling. In truth, there wasn't much of a difference between the floor of the casino and the market, with pipe dreams influencing monetary decisions. Henry was stepping ahead of the curve by applying numbers, and in 1981 he established his own investment firm, which Rzepczynski would later preside over, John W. Henry & Company.

That year, 5,000 miles away, Liverpool lifted their third European Cup – now known as the Champions League – in Paris under the leadership of Bob Paisley, who was experiencing his seventh successive campaign in charge of the Reds. Football was different in those days. Much like the world of business that Henry was enduring at the time, decisions on and off the pitch were shaped by rudimentary feelings and pure instinct. The tactical elements of the game were largely overlooked, with players instructed to go and win what was essentially a battle of will rather than a complex sport that would later embrace strategy. 'Work it out for yourself, son,' was a term used on a regular basis before matches, according to Graeme Souness, who once testified to asking for instructions just minutes before his first-team debut at Liverpool, only to be shamed by Paisley's assistant, Joe Fagan. 'We've paid all this money for you, and you're asking me how to play football,' he said.

Souness, who captained the team for a two-year spell in the 80s, has since elaborated on how Liverpool rarely held team meetings or talked about their opponents during his time as a player at the club. A matter of hours before the European Cup Final in 1984, Fagan, who had succeeded Paisley to become manager, addressed his players after eating lunch at their hotel in Rome. The Walton-born Scouser rattled his glass with a spoon to gather the attention of those surrounding him in an uncharacteristic move. Silence consumed the room, before he stood up to give an unexpected but brief speech. 'Big game tonight, boys,' he said in a nonchalant tone, unruffled by the event. 'They must be a good team, but they can't be as good as us. They can't be as good as us. The bus leaves at 5.30pm, don't be late.' Preparation was simple and borderline prehistoric, but it was normal. Nobody expected much more. Liverpool won the final by four goals to two on penalties; football was straightforward.

There was a vague tactical identity at Anfield at the time, and it was considered as far more advanced than most of Liverpool's domestic rivals. The team upheld a possession-based playing style that had been shaped by their exploits in Europe. Liverpool's tie in the second round of the European Cup against Red Star Belgrade in 1973 was a particular catalyst for change upon reflection of the club's history, having had a dramatic impact on their approach after Bill Shankly's men lost both legs by a combined score of four goals to two. The central defenders of Red Star caught the attention of Paisley, who was Shankly's assistant at the time. They behaved like midfielders when in possession of the ball, demonstrating a capacity to pass through the thirds of the pitch without panicking or making unforced errors. Rather than hitting long to a physical striker and attempting to penetrate the penalty box with every single touch in a perfectly English fashion, the Red Star defenders remained composed and progressed through Liverpool using passing triangles.

It was different from the football witnessed back home. Aggressive and rugged defenders were fielded on English shores. It was all about dying before ever conceding a goal; what you did in possession didn't matter so much. After witnessing the future against the champions of Yugoslavia, Liverpool experimented in an attempt to copy Red Star by deploying midfielder Phil Thompson in the centre of defence alongside Emlyn Hughes, who had experience as a full-back and as a midfielder, rather than Tommy Smith and Larry Lloyd, who featured in both legs and seemed to suit a more direct style of play. 'The Europeans showed that building from the back is the only way to play. When they play the ball from the back, they play in little groups,' Shankly later recalled. 'We realised at Liverpool that you can't score a goal every time you get the ball. And we learned this from Europe, from the Latin people. It started in Europe and we adapted it into our game.' Liverpool gained an edge over their domestic rivals on the back of their contests on the continent, but tactical concepts back then were still largely undeveloped in comparison to modern times. The pitch was more of a war zone than a chess board.

If the tactical landscape of football was to be described as undeveloped back then, statistical conditions could be deemed as almost embryonic. Data relating to the performances of players and teams was simply not recorded by those competing in the sport, largely because the required technology hadn't yet been invented. In the eyes of many people within the game, nothing mattered beyond the numbers that formed the league table, consisting of columns such as wins, draws, losses, goals scored and goals conceded. Goal difference, an ordinary calculation of goals scored minus goals conceded, is now mainstream and widely considered as commonplace, but it wasn't introduced as a tiebreaker in association football until the 1970s. Before that, goal average was the go-to formula, a broken metric that epitomised the lack of expertise surrounding the use of numbers in football at the time. Goal average consisted of the number of goals scored divided by the number conceded, which naturally favoured conservative playing styles rather than encouraging offensive football and entertainment, and it was eventually scrapped.

Data didn't exist beyond manual collection, which was first reportedly conducted by Charles Reep in 1950. Reep was mathematically inclined and suited his role serving as an accountant for the Royal Air Force. Located in London due to his services, Reep occasionally attended Arsenal and Tottenham Hotspur matches up until a clash between Swindon Town and Bristol Rovers forced him to begin analysing the inner workings of the game. At half-time, he was bemused by the brand of football that he was witnessing, is how the famous tale goes, with the home team adopting a lethargic and ineffective approach when in possession of the ball. It was all sideways, there was no practicality. He had been consumed by boredom, so for the next 45 minutes Reep used a notepad to record a portion of basic events on the pitch, particularly those associated with passing sequences and how attacking plays ended, of which there were 147 according to his count.

He began dedicating his time towards recording data, watching roughly 40 matches per season and spending 80 hours per match noting down his figures. The standard of technological advancement at the time was captured by Reep having to wear a miner's helmet to make notes during night matches, using the light on his head to illuminate his pad. He couldn't use an iPhone, laptop or tablet, this was the Stone Age. Once delving into the data that he had collected over time, Reep began exploring analytics before it was a thing, attempting to interpret patterns in his numbers and using those to deliver strategic insights. His analysis concluded that lengthy sequences of possession failed to add much value and that, instead, moves that consisted of three passes or fewer delivered the most goals. His claim, in essence, was that long-ball football was more effective, as he told the BBC in 1993. 'If a team tries to play football and keeps it down to no more than three passes, it will have a much higher chance of winning matches,' he said. 'Passing for the sake of passing can be disastrous.'

While Reep might have had a point with the closing line of his statement, his analysis was primarily flawed. He identified that a larger proportion of goals happened on the back of short sequences, but without considering whether such a finding had a direct association with the actual probability of scoring. Football, particularly during Reep's era, was akin to basketball in the sense that turnovers happened frequently and possession bounced from one end of the pitch to the other every few seconds. It was chaos. He was keen to challenge the worth of lengthy sequences but, ultimately, those sequences didn't happen that often anyway.

Reep's analysis was not wholly objective, and his findings seemed to be shaped by an underlying innate belief that related back to his boredom when watching Swindon Town against Bristol Rovers. Nevertheless, his efforts did prove to be enough to gain him paid work in football. He operated as a consultant for Stan Cullis, manager of Wolverhampton Wanderers, for three and a half years before retiring from the Royal Air Force and assuming a role as an analyst for Sheffield Wednesday. He helped over 20 clubs during his career as the first of his kind, encouraging each of them to adopt a direct and vertical playing style that discouraged square passes and ball retention.

In many ways, his emergence as Britain's first football analyst shaped how the game would evolve in England for years to come, as his work was picked up further down the line by a man named Charles Hughes, who would later end up becoming director of coaching for the English Football Association. Although he denied being inspired by Reep, Hughes held a similar perspective on the game, stating that 85 per cent of goals were scored from moves of five passes or fewer in his book, *The Winning Formula*.

The evidence-based beliefs held by Reep influenced styles up and down the country as players were instructed to almost bypass the centre of the field in favour of lofted passes towards the penalty area. The two penalty boxes at both ends of the pitch mattered most; everything else was just noise as Reep searched for a signal in his data. 'Passing has become such a fetish that one sometimes has the impression that goal-scoring has become the secondary objective,' he said, with regular condemnation aimed in the direction of what he labelled as 'continental' and 'cultured' styles of football, which is what Liverpool had steadily began to adopt on the back of their consecutive defeats to Red Star on Europe's biggest stage.

Reep was ahead of his time. A trailblazer for football analytics 50 years before data was treated as scarcely useful by those competing at the pinnacle of the sport. He believed in a specific style of play and – unlike a whole host of coaches to influence football over the decades – he was committed to proving that his was the most practical and effective by supporting his case with substantial evidence rather than ego and plain opinion. He might have argued that numbers cannot lie, but while that's technically true, the figures are open to the interpretation of the user and how that user translates them. The quality of the data matters, as does the sample size. Data continues to be shunned by sections of people surrounding football in the present day, and that lack of trust tends to stem from how numbers can be easily manipulated. They can support virtually any argument. Incorrect and damaging conclusions can be drawn by those who are uninitiated or negligent, with Reep and Hughes partially responsible for impeding the early development of English football in comparison to the likes of Italy, Germany, Spain and the

Netherlands, who prospered on the international stage more often. 'Football is a simple game, complicated by idiots,' Shankly once said, but Reep would likely have suggested otherwise.

As an inquisitive St Louis Cardinals fan who grew up calculating baseball percentages while listening to radio commentary, John Henry was bound to recognise and exploit the endless opportunities in the world of sport at some stage. He saw nothing but inefficiencies, waiting to be attacked and optimised. As he was conquering the business world, he tested the water on numerous occasions, including his purchase of a one per cent stake in the New York Yankees, which coincided with Kenny Dalglish's resignation from the managerial hot seat at Anfield after almost six years in charge between 1985 and 1991. Eight years later, Henry purchased the Florida Marlins from Wayne Huizenga, who had proved to be a difficult person to negotiate with after repeatedly changing the terms of the sale despite reaching a verbal agreement. 'This has been a dream I've had for a long time,' Henry said after securing the $150m purchase, with his immediate responsibility as owner surrounding a deal for a new baseball-only stadium for the Marlins. Huizenga had encountered problems when attempting to strike a deal for a stadium, and that was part of the reason behind his decision to sell.

Henry would make strides forward at the beginning of his ownership by reaching a stadium agreement with City of Miami officials, but after experiencing a series of setbacks and struggling to finalise a deal, he sold the club three years later to acquire the Boston Red Sox as part of a newly founded group named New England Sports

Ventures, which would later become Fenway Sports Group (FSG). Tom Werner, a successful TV producer, joined forces with Henry alongside Les Otten, The New York Times Company and other investors to form the collective, with a deal pushed over the line in 2002.

It was time for Henry's sporting expedition to properly begin. He would attempt to achieve success in the world of baseball using the same methodology that had delivered rewards in business, by placing unwavering faith in the power of numbers and gaining an edge over competitors by thinking about gaining an upper hand, just like he did at the blackjack tables in Vegas. Baseball was far more familiar with data than football, with statistics forming an integral part of the sport that revolved around nothing but set-pieces from start to finish. Everything could be quantified, and collecting data was relatively easy in comparison to other more free-flowing sports that simply didn't allow for time to breathe. The absence of numbers in baseball wasn't the underlying problem in Henry's eyes. The inefficiency lay in the data that was generally deemed to be valuable, with some of the sport's most beloved metrics disguised as meaningful, when in practice they divulged very little about performance in relation to acquiring wins. A storied term would eventually be fashioned to loosely define the practices applied by Henry's ownership in Boston: 'Moneyball'.

Chapter Two

The Big Bang

OVERCOMING THE loss of your best player can be difficult. It's an inconvenience that has impacted even the most glamorous and famous teams in the world across multiple different sports. Such a happening can enforce times of hardship upon a team, with the duration of the rebalancing process equating to fewer wins on the pitch and, occasionally, a trophy drought.

The world of football runs in cycles according to Alex Ferguson, who regularly used the term during his 26-year spell in charge of Manchester United, and the numerous eras of dominance in the Champions League since it was first established as European football's leading competition in 1955 reinforce his point. Spain's Real Madrid won the first five tournaments, followed by a two-year spell at the pinnacle for Portugal's Benfica, before the trophy spent three years in Italy as AC Milan and Inter Milan prospered. The Netherlands had their time in the sun between 1969 and 1973, winning the trophy four times in a row through Ajax and Feyenoord, with three consecutive wins for Germany's Bayern Munich following, before England's boom finally arrived. In the eight years between 1976 and 1984, the trophy was won by an English team seven times, including four Liverpool triumphs. Italy returned to the top between 1988 and 1998 thanks to Serie A's golden era, with at least one Italian outfit featuring in all but two of the ten finals throughout that period, and the same applies to English clubs between 2004 and 2009. La Liga is the most recent major league to govern the tournament, with Real Madrid reclaiming their age-old crown by winning four of the five competitions between 2013 and 2018 – and another in 2022 – although now the immortal pairing of Cristiano Ronaldo and Lionel Messi have departed Spain for new shores, English clubs could be next to seize the throne.

Those cycles can last forever from the perspectives of the clubs waiting to step into the light but, in reality, the footballing landscape is always changing and fostering new champions. Even Europe's most prominent clubs can drift from the summit, but it rarely takes longer than a couple of decades at most for normality to return, which is more than can be said for the Boston Red Sox. The drought at Fenway Park had spiralled into something more than a classic dry spell upon John Henry's takeover. It had snowballed over time to become what was widely labelled as a curse that coincided with the loss of George Herman Ruth Jr – better known as Babe Ruth – in 1919. The Christmas period of that year wasn't celebrated by the residents of Boston. The Red Sox made a controversial decision on Boxing Day to allow Ruth to join the New York Yankees for a hefty $100,000. He was the ultimate festive present for supporters in the Big Apple to unwrap.

Ruth had formed part of three championship-winning outfits for the Red Sox during a spell in which they won five of the first 15 World Series titles. He was a left-handed pitcher, but one who also had an innate ability for hitting balls out of the park. Ruth towered over most of his team-mates at around 6ft 2in tall, and his swing was much like his character: brazen, free and chancy. A keen gambler with a liberated but flawed nature, Ruth was a difficult person to manage due to his volatility and capriciousness. He drank, committed traffic violations, skipped practice and complained when things didn't go his way, but his team-mates persisted because of his brilliance on the field. He made the difference. Weighing over 200lbs, Ruth was troublesome, excellent and one of a kind. In a footballing sense, he depicted shades of Paul Gascoigne, George Best and Diego Maradona. For all his defects, he was worth the hassle, and he knew it.

Ruth recognised his worth before too long and began to favour flashy home runs as opposed to pitching, but the Red Sox wanted him to focus on the latter and showered him with bonuses to appease him. It was a temporary solution that led to Ruth demanding his salary be doubled by Harry Frazee, who owned the Red Sox at the time. Ruth used a series of negotiation tactics to get his way – some more audacious than others – including missing games and threatening to abandon his beloved sport to explore a new-found interest in boxing. Frazee, who was a theatrical producer, was concerned with debt and couldn't meet Ruth's excessive and growing requests. He eventually succumbed to his trade for the good of the team according to his own reasoning, but in doing so Frazee inadvertently initiated a change in fortune between the Red Sox and the Yankees, who hadn't yet won a World Series.

The Hollywood signature of Ruth would shape how the Yankees operated in future, after he helped to deliver four World Series titles over the next 15 seasons as a full-time outfielder, breaking his own record for home runs in a single campaign several times. The extravagant and high-profile transfer was born. The Yankees began to pave a way that Real Madrid would follow decades later in the footballing world, establishing their own 'Galactico' recruitment policy in Europe by signing superstars such as Zinedine Zidane, David Beckham, Luís Figo and Ronaldo for sky-high transfer fees. Between 2000 and 2013, Madrid broke their own world transfer record five times. In New York, Ruth was an outstanding success for the Yankees. He was nicknamed 'Bambino' by the Italian communities within the city, which translated into baby, or in Ruth's case, 'Babe'. Henry's assignment as owner of the Red Sox was not only to conquer the stardom-fuelled Yankees, but it was also to break a hex that had lingered in Boston for almost a century.

The year that FSG's takeover was finalised, a lightweight team named the Oakland Athletics finished top of the American League West despite running on a relatively shoestring budget, especially in comparison to the Yankees, whose payroll was around three times larger. In the build-up to their famous 2002 season, the As had lost three of their best players in Jason Giambi, Jason Isringhausen and Johnny Damon, the first of whom joined the prestigious Yankees. Billy Beane was general manager of the As at the time, a former player who was tipped for greatness by scouts at the beginning of his playing career, only to ultimately fall short of those lofty expectations. Frustrated by the unfair playing field and the financial limitations of the As, Beane tackled the voids within his squad by attempting to break the mould. He was keen to challenge conventional wisdom, aware of the cruel advantages held by other teams. Paul DePodesta was central to Beane's new thought process. An economics graduate from Harvard University, DePodesta was poached from the Cleveland Indians to work as Beane's assistant, and after conflicting with scouting director Grady Fuson over opinions regarding players, DePodesta and Beane decided to navigate their roster problem using sabermetrics, a concept formulated and promoted by Bill James.

A dedicated baseball fan who worked as a security guard at the time, James began writing data-driven articles about his favourite sport in his mid-20s, offering novel insights that were reinforced by numbers. The aspiring writer had found a niche, but one that was too peculiar for most editors to accept, forcing James to publish his own work in book form, the first of which was released in 1977. The Kansas-born fanatic had formed bold opinions on baseball relating to how the game should be played to achieve optimal results, and although his work was thorough and detailed, his conclusions could be simplified. 'The key to scoring runs in baseball is getting people on base,' said James when describing the crux of his fundamental case, which conflicted with how the sport was played on the field. 'For a long time, people wanted to de-emphasise that and argue that you can score just as many runs by stealing bases and those sorts of things.

Well, stealing bases adds some runs but very few, and you lose most of the runs that you gain by having runners caught stealing. The way you really score more runs is by getting more people on base,' said James.

He initially struggled to popularise his studies, but persistence – alongside a timely profile of his work in *Sports Illustrated* – allowed him to gain a degree of recognition. Baseball was a sport familiar with statistics, but James had precise views on which numbers were valuable, and which numbers had a lesser importance within the context of delivering wins. On-base percentage (OBP) – which refers to how frequently a batter reaches base – was more meaningful than mainstream stats such as batting average, bunts and stolen bases according to his research. Beane and DePodesta recognised that the value associated with a player's OBP wasn't always reflected in his salary. It was an undervalued element of player evaluation, whereas the players who hit the hardest – known as sluggers – were commonly overvalued.

James's logic was applied by the As in their pursuit of new talent, with Beane taking chances on several players to fill the gaps in the team. David Justice was one of the additions who was deemed to be a risk. He was 36 years old and past his peak, but was labelled as an 'experiment' by DePodesta. Could an ageing player retain his ability to get on base? The As wanted to find out. Scott Hatteberg was another player who was picked up on the back of his respectable OBP, despite his role as a catcher. He had encountered issues when throwing due to an elbow injury, but the plan was to retrain him as a first baseman to harvest his ability to get on base.

The As bettered their regular season record from the previous year in that 2002 campaign, despite losing the likes of Giambi. It was a triumph, but one that was overshadowed by their winning of 20 consecutive matches between 13 August and 4 September, which was an American League record. Hatteberg, the team's newborn hitter, decided the 20th contest by hitting a celebrated home run into the stands. So memorable was the season for the As that a book was released by Michael Lewis shortly after. He was afforded the luxury of closely following the team throughout the campaign. *Moneyball: The Art of Winning an Unfair Game* exploded to have a serious impact on the sport. 'The As figured out that OBP was the single most important statistic in evaluating a hitter, and that it was most closely correlated with the scoring of runs,' said Lewis when talking about the story behind his book. 'The old way of evaluating players was simply by looking at them,' he added. 'The scouts looked, made judgements and told you what to do. The As were paying a lot less attention to their scouts than other teams. Instead, they availed themselves to a body of research and development that had originated from outside of baseball.'

The book was later transformed into a motion picture, less than a decade after it was released. Brad Pitt was the actor who was cast as Beane, receiving two Oscar nominations for Best Picture and Best Actor for his performance in the role. Throughout the film, Pitt captured the essence of Beane's appetite to challenge the status quo through his use of subtle yet shrewd remarks. 'If we try to play like the Yankees in here, we will lose to the Yankees out there,' he said in a defining scene with his scouting department. 'What is the problem?' he asked in one scene, with two scouts referencing the need to replace Giambi, Isringhausen and Damon in their answers. 'The problem,' he clarified, 'is that there are rich teams, and there are poor teams, then there's 50 feet of crap, and then there's us. It's an unfair game.'

Alongside Pitt's characterisation of Beane, Jonah Hill was cast as DePodesta. Named as Peter Brand in the film due to DePodesta's request for anonymity, Hill portrayed the ultimate boffin whose introverted personality and pudgy appearance conflicted with those of scouts and players in the sport. Hill represented an exaggerated version of DePodesta in the film, who had actually played football and baseball while studying at Harvard, but he too was capable of encapsulating alternative thinking by using understated remarks. 'It's about getting things down to one number,' Hill says to Pitt in one scene. 'Using stats the way we read them, we'll find value in players that nobody else can see. People are overlooked for a variety of biased reasons and perceived flaws: age, appearance, personality. Bill James and mathematics cut straight through that.'

On the back of the book's success, the underlying sporting lesson of *Moneyball* has almost been lost in translation, although to an extent it was always open to interpretation in the first place. It has a million different messages. Some believe *Moneyball* showed how to find ways to win through innovation, whereas others suggest that it was about acquiring the undervalued and discarding the overvalued. It has also been hailed as the showpiece that highlighted the value of including data in a player recruitment process. In a conversation with Matt Addison of the *Liverpool Echo*, Beane defined the concept as the applied use of objective analysis to decisions, and finding inefficiencies in different markets. All in all, *Moneyball* can be accurately described as a cocktail of each of those things.

Towards the end of the film, Beane meets with John Henry in the stands of Fenway Park. 'For $41m, you built a play-off team. You lost Damon, Giambi and Isringhausen, and you won more games without them than you did with them,' said Henry, who was played by Arliss Howard, in the scene. 'You won the exact same number of games that the Yankees won. Anybody who isn't tearing their team down and rebuilding it using your model, they're dinosaurs. I want you to be my general manager.' In a scene that visualised a real-life discussion, Henry offered Beane $12.5m to become the highest-paid general manager ever but, remarkably, he declined. 'I got to watch my daughter grow up,' said Beane years after denying the Red Sox. 'She's 27 now, but I was there and I didn't miss a thing.'

You can't believe everything that you see, hear or read in Hollywood. Everybody loves a fairytale with a happy ending or a hero who saves the day with precision timing, but that isn't how real life usually works. Stories are fabricated for the big screen. Contrary to the message projected in *Jaws*, sharks aren't actually that much of a threat to people enjoying beaches. In fact, dogs tend to kill more people every year than sharks do, and considering *Braveheart* is loosely based on the story of a 13th-century Scottish leader, kilts technically weren't around back then. Unfortunately, the same applies to *Moneyball*. Much like Hill's extravagant portrayal of DePodesta – who actually joined the As in 1999 rather than 2002 as suggested in the film – the drama and accuracy of *Moneyball* has been challenged on the back of its global popularity. The As were painted as having achieved relative success purely on the back of Beane's canny acquisitions, which doesn't tell the full story. There have always been further layers to the tale.

The little attention that was given to the team's starting pitchers is considered as one of the major issues with the story told by Lewis. Few words were dedicated to Mark Mulder, Tim Hudson and Barry Zito in the book, despite the trio making significant contributions to how the As managed to win games. Mulder, Hudson and Zito were early-round draft picks, but they didn't fit the overriding concept of *Moneyball*, hence Lewis's decision to mention their names just 32 times in total in his book. 'What Oakland won they didn't win because of sabermetrics. They won because of Mulder, Hudson, Zito and Miguel Tejada,' said former relief pitcher Mitch Williams. Tejada was the league MVP in 2002, and rather than joining as a product of recruitment charged by sabermetrics, he was picked up by a scout while playing in the Dominican Republic. He made his professional debut for the As in 1997, and by 2002 he was recognised as one of the league's best performers.

His rise conflicted with one of the main narratives of *Moneyball*, relating to Beane's difficult relationship with traditional scouts on the back of his past experiences as a youngster in the game. 'Billy had been on the receiving end of the intuitive judgements of scouts,' said Lewis after writing his book. 'The scouts all said this guy was going to be a future superstar and basically talked him out of going to college, so I think he is still slightly hostile with scouts.' Hatteberg, who was Beane's very own catcher-turned-hitter and was mentioned 121 times in Lewis's book, was bought for $900,000 by the As. His capture was a stroke of genius, but Beane had to pay him around $2.5m to leave after three seasons, which hardly reflects the 'Moneyball' mantra of buying low and selling high. Giambi, the pricey slugger who left for the Yankees, was replaced by reliable OBP agents like Hatteberg and Justice, but as time progressed subsequent to the release of Lewis's book, Beane struggled to uphold the As offensive game by acquiring worthy contributors.

'The team that seems to have benefited most from the study of sabermetrics is the Boston Red Sox,' wrote Allen Barra for *The Atlantic*. While John Henry failed in his bid to land Beane as his general manager, his longing to establish a scientific institution was unperturbed. It was merely a minor setback. To navigate the problem of Beane refusing the Red Sox, Henry simply hired Bill James as his senior baseball adviser. He wasn't obliged to move to Boston, and rather than working as a scout, James would operate as a consultant of sorts, helping within the organisation whenever required. Henry likened his own data-powered business practices to those of James in the baseball world. 'Actual data from the market means more than individual perception,' Henry said. 'The same is true in baseball. I just happened to apply quantitative analysis to an area that's extremely lucrative.'

With James on board as an adviser, Henry still required a disciple of his work to steer the ship in Boston, and he found one in Theo Epstein. A fresh-faced Yale graduate who was just 28 years old at the time, Epstein was a lawyer with no experience as a baseball player or as a coach. Larry Lucchino, the team's president, was largely responsible for Epstein's hire. He had worked with him in Baltimore and San Diego before bringing him to Boston, but there was still an element of risk attached to his appointment. He was different from his peers. Epstein hadn't been shaped by the sport like Beane and other familiar faces. He looked like an accountant and had previously worked in public relations, but proved to have a knack for marrying analytics with intuition. Epstein was a pupil of James's musings, which he used as a framework when making decisions surrounding the Red Sox roster.

Just two years after Henry, James, Epstein and the new regime descended on Boston, the so-called 'Curse of the Bambino' was broken. The Red Sox won the World Series in 2004 and, just for good measure, they won it again in 2007. 'The Red Sox are like the As, but with money,' said Stephen Moyer, former president of Baseball Info Solutions, a sabermetrics company. Epstein inherited a solid foundation at Fenway Park, but he strengthened by picking up players who would go down in history, such as David Ortiz, while controversially cutting ties with dwindling stars such as Nomar Garciaparra. In an article for *The Athletic* in 2022, Jen McCaffrey and Chad Jennings wrote:

> The Red Sox have experienced more success in the past two decades than in the previous century, and the franchise's turning point is unmistakable: the arrival of a new ownership

group, led by John Henry, that officially took over 20 years ago this spring training. In business and on the field, the organisation has become a model franchise, imperfect but prosperous, with much of its newfound success rooted in the introduction of a collaborative, open-minded culture that was ahead of its time.

The Red Sox were 'light years ahead' of the competition according to James:

> Analytics is not done with statistics, it's done by applying scientific methods to real-life problems. We work with statistics in the same way that any other science does, the same way that economics or biology does. The people in the first wave of analytics in baseball, 2006 to 2007, mostly did not have any understanding of that, so they mostly didn't get anything out of it. Nobody else was [doing it], period.

Despite the hyperbole and storytelling elements attached to *Moneyball*, the morals of the tale made waves that reshaped the sporting landscape, especially in the US. Speaking about the influence of his book years later, Lewis recalled phone calls with people who had witnessed owners walking into executive offices holding paperback copies of *Moneyball* in their hands. Over time, OBP started getting widely recognised as a valuable metric, meaning it was no longer overlooked by those identifying talent. 'In the last few years since *Moneyball*, OBP has become very fashionable and Beane would tell you that it's become overpriced,' said Lewis. Indeed, Beane told the *Washington Post* exactly that in 2018. 'Teams are valuing the same things. The big teams are run very wisely now, it's a very intelligent industry,' he said.

Moneyball eventually transcended the sport of baseball to such an extent that basketball wanted a slice of the analytics pie, with Daryl Morey appointed as general manager of the Houston Rockets in 2007. Like Theo Epstein in Boston, Morey didn't fit the traditional form of his peers. The computer science and statistics graduate had never played the sport in a professional capacity, but that actually proved to be an advantage. Morey was a nerd for numbers. In fact, he read about Bill James and his early takes on baseball as a 16-year-old. Charles Barkley, an 11-time NBA All-Star, was one of Morey's most public doubters. 'He's one of those idiots who believe in analytics,' Barkley famously said. 'I've always believed analytics was crap. The NBA is about talent. All these guys who run these organisations who talk about analytics, they have one thing in common. They're a bunch of guys who ain't never played the game, and they never got the girls in high school and they just want to get in the game.' His criticism was brutal, but ultimately wrong. Morey's ideas would wind up having quite the impression on how the sport would evolve on the court.

The three-pointer was his hallmark. 'It's pretty dramatic how powerful the three-point shot is,' said Morey as he discouraged the Rockets from attempting shots from inside the two-point zone. Statistically, long two-point shots originating from just inside the three-point line were identified as providing the worst return. Shooting from beyond the three-point line was far more beneficial. To maximise the points scored by the Rockets per possession, he fostered a three-point culture that was powered by evidence and analytics. Shooting from further out was a risk, but it was worth the reward because the pay-off was 50 per cent greater. In footballing terms, imagine a goal scored from inside the penalty box was worth one goal, whereas one scored from outside the penalty box was worth 1.5 goals. It would certainly make players and coaches think.

The number of attempted three-point shots in the NBA has increased every year for the past decade. When Michael Jordan made his NBA debut appearance in 1984, he would have witnessed fewer than five three-point attempts per match compared to over 30 per match in the present day. Three-point shots are more efficient. They're more optimal, and the Rockets effectively started the movement. In fact, they made more three-point shots than any other team in NBA history in their 2018/19 campaign, bettering their previous record from the season before. During Morey's spell in Houston from 2007 to 2020, the Rockets recorded the second-best overall record in the NBA. The term 'Moreyball' was expertly fashioned on the back of his methods, and Lewis called attention to his story through the release of a new book in 2016, *The Undoing Project*.

As the data-charged Big Bang stimulated the rapid expansion of science and mathematics throughout American sports, football was slow to catch on. The roots of the beautiful game are found in Europe and, for too long, they remained detached and removed from new ideas emerging from faraway sources. Basic data, on the other hand, did manage to seep into football, with Opta founded six years before the As experienced their 'Moneyball' season in 2002. After being contracted by Sky Sports to support their television broadcasts, Opta became the official statistics provider for the Premier League in 1997, which was known as the Premiership at the time. The data collection that was being undertaken was revolutionary, but relatively primordial compared to modern practices, largely because of technological limitations. Opta began collecting real-time data in 1999, before making individual player data available one year later. Football was advancing, but years would pass before numbers truly began informing recruitment and strategic decisions on the pitch.

The first high-profile breakthrough happened at Manchester United, who embraced the assistance of Prozone through Steve McClaren. He was hired as Alex Ferguson's assistant in 1999 and arrived with prior knowledge of Prozone due to his previous coaching role at Derby County. The cutting-edge product was created by Ramm Mylvaganam, who wasn't much of a football fan but, thanks to McClaren, was afforded the opportunity to explore and create his innovative concept. Six hi-tech cameras were installed at Pride Park. They would track the movements of each player on the pitch every 0.1 seconds, allowing for new-age analysis. A simulator-like bunker was erected at Derby's training ground, consisting of distinctive chairs that Mylvaganam had previously been responsible for selling while working for a consultancy group. The chairs aided recovery by vibrating and oscillating to send pulses through muscles. McClaren was receptive and resourceful as a young coach, and his openness to Prozone captured his visionary perspective. Once he had been poached by Ferguson he wanted to bring Prozone with him. His request was accepted, although United were reluctant to pay for the services of the unproven product. 'We're Manchester United. We don't pay people, people pay us,' said the club's CEO, David Gill, before agreeing to a £50,000 deal providing the club won a trophy at the end of the season. By the following summer, United had won the treble, securing the Premier League, FA Cup and Champions League.

'Prozone went into the stratosphere because Ole Gunnar Solskjær scored that goal in the Nou Camp. Without that, nobody would have heard of us,' Mylvaganam told the *Manchester Evening News*. The silverware was the proof, and United's success understandably resulted in widespread interest in Prozone. 'We had two clients in May of 1999 in United and Derby,' said Mylvaganam. 'By August, we had six clients with all of them paying, except for Derby. It was the moment it took off.' A queue had formed for the services of Prozone on the back of United's success, but it was little more than a box-ticking exercise for the most part. A whole host of clubs gained access to the product because of how important it was deemed to be, but few used it. The notion of using data to improve performance had been introduced, but the sport as a whole remained sceptical. 'Football was late to wake up to data,' Mylvaganam later told *The Athletic*.

Liverpool had the opportunity to get ahead of their competitors in 2007, becoming only the third club in the

Premier League to be acquired by American investors, behind United and Aston Villa. David Moores owned 51 per cent of Liverpool at the time, but the club needed more substantial investment to compete with the likes of Roman Abramovich, who was in the process of remodelling Chelsea using his unrivalled wealth. After Moores rejected a deal with Thaksin Shinawatra in 2004 – who later bought Manchester City – he formally accepted a joint offer from Tom Hicks and George Gillett. The pair promised a new stadium and funds to be made available in the transfer market. 'If Rafa [Benítez] said he wanted to buy Snoogy Doogy, we would back him,' was one of their famous sound bites, but the humorous comment would offer a glimpse into the expertise that was to come. They were American, and they had a background in sports, but Hicks and Gillett were amateurs.

Chapter Three

Cowboys

WHEN LIVERPOOL signed John Barnes in 1987 he was surprised upon attending his first training session at Melwood. 'When I first went to Liverpool, there was no coaching at all,' he said. 'You had great players with great experience and expected a certain level of consistency. I went there having been an international for five years, but when a new group of young players came through, they needed coaching. I think Liverpool fell behind.' The Merseyside club had won six of the last ten English top-flight titles prior to signing Barnes, but such dominance seemed to foster complacency. It had always worked in the past, so it will work again in the future, was the line of thinking. It was hardly a surprise that by the time the First Division was rebranded as the Premiership in 1992, the decline of the Reds had begun.

By the turn of the century, the best finish Liverpool had achieved in the Premier League era was third, in 1995/96 and 1997/98. They had slipped into a relatively strange but almost satisfactory space, winning cup competitions fairly often but all while falling short of reclaiming their coveted English crown. Steven Gerrard, Michael Owen, Jamie Carragher, Steve McManaman and Robbie Fowler shone as local favourites who had graduated from the club's academy to lift meaningful trophies. Liverpool won the FA Cup, UEFA Cup, UEFA Super Cup, and the League Cup twice under Gérard Houllier between 1998 and 2004, who was educated as a teacher and possessed an instinctive eye for spotting relatively unknown prodigies. Later in his career, Houllier would have an instrumental impact on the journeys of Sadio Mané and Naby Keïta, having advised Red Bull Salzburg to sign the pair from Metz and FC Istres before they moved to Anfield further down the line.

Houllier's best Premier League finish was second in 2001/02, seven points behind Arsène Wenger's ultra-modern Arsenal. Liverpool had spirit, fortitude and character in abundance under his leadership, but the team's playing style was largely cautious and functional throughout his tenure. The Frenchman was known for his management of people rather than his tactical acumen, which was deemed as not so important at the time, given the fashion of 4-4-2 as the favoured formation of English football. At one stage, Houllier's defensive line consisted of four centre-backs in Carragher, Sami Hyypiä, Stéphane Henchoz and Markus Babbel. The more offensive John Arne Riise ousted Babbel when Liverpool finished second in the table, but Houllier's safety-first approach remained. 'It was like a wall of 6ft players who were all aggressive,' said Gary Neville, who lined up as an opponent for Manchester United several times, in a conversation with Carragher. 'There wasn't a massive amount of football coming out from the back, but it was solid back-four defending,' he said. Carragher agreed, describing Houllier as a 'defensive manager' who wanted a back four that 'didn't shift, and didn't move'. Liverpool ended the season with the best defensive record in the division when they finished as runners-up, but they scored 20 goals fewer than Alex Ferguson's Manchester United and 12 fewer than Arsenal.

Wenger's team in particular showcased football that was cultured and almost futuristic. He was wise, creative and arrived from Japan with groundbreaking plans to overhaul fitness and nutrition. He had studied physiology earlier in his career, so brought in dieticians to communicate the benefits of eating pasta, boiled chicken, steamed fish and raw vegetables as opposed to junk food. Water was recommended, and casual drinking – which was an ingrained part of English culture – was banned. Nicknamed 'Le Professeur', Wenger favoured 4-4-2 like the rest, but his players occupied unconventional spaces once possession was secured, and the ways in which Arsenal attacked seemed to separate them from the pack.

Robert Pires and Freddie Ljungberg were fielded as wingers on paper, but rather than hugging the touchline and hitting repeated crosses into the penalty box like other wide players, the pair drifted inside and bagged their fair share of goals. When the latter originally signed for Arsenal in 1998 he scored a goal from outside the box during an early training session, hoping to impress his boss in the process. Wenger wasn't particularly thrilled. In fact, he stopped the training session at the time and informed Ljungberg in front of his team-mates that shooting from such far out locations wasn't an accepted practice at

Highbury. 'In this team, we pass it,' he said. 'You do not shoot from there.'

Dennis Bergkamp was one of the team's two strikers, but he operated in deeper areas between the lines of the opposition's midfield and defence. Signed in 1995, Bergkamp embodied a new trend that involved a pure goalscorer teaming up with a more supportive partner who would make withdrawn movements away from goal, dropping into more advanced midfield spaces. He painted himself as a genius who could have a subtle yet dramatic impact on proceedings, as a connector of sorts who was one step ahead of everybody else around him. United's version of Bergkamp was Eric Cantona, and Liverpool eventually jumped on the bandwagon in January 2001, signing a 29-year-old version of Jari Litmanen on a free transfer from Barcelona. As usual, the Reds were late to the party. Liverpool didn't set trends, they followed them.

Above all, Arsenal demonstrated a greater intent than most to control the element of chance on the pitch. Keeping the ball suddenly mattered. Wenger placed less of an emphasis on crossing – given the nature of his inverted wingers – and shooting from distance, and Arsenal became known for their fluidity and class, passing the ball through the tightest of spaces and working the ball as close to the goal as possible before attempting to score. The Gunners highlighted the lack of sense associated with getting the ball into the penalty box by any means necessary. They weren't perfect and Wenger didn't necessarily have a scientific background influencing his tactical methods, but Arsenal's game naturally sided with probability. 'Winning should be the result of the quality of your playing style and how you express yourself on the pitch,' he once said. 'All my life, people have told me that we need to win on Saturday. As a coach, I know that, but how?'

Two seasons after Liverpool finished second, Arsenal became known as 'Invincibles' by winning the Premier League without losing a single match in the process. Houllier was supposed to be Liverpool's own version of Wenger, with the Reds again following trends rather than setting them. He was French, soft-spoken, wise and collected, just like the man in charge of the Gunners. He was successful in bringing the Merseyside club into the 20th century by modernising key departments, but he fell short of glory in the Premier League and Champions League.

When Houllier left the club in 2004, Liverpool had a mixed bag of replacements on their shortlist, from Alan Curbishley to José Mourinho to Martin O'Neill, but Rafael Benítez was eventually awarded the job after his fine work at Valencia. The Spaniard made Liverpool even less expressive than Houllier but, unlike his predecessor, he was an elite tactician and prioritised strategy and organisation above keeping the morale of his players high. Benítez appeared cold and almost robotic from a distance. He refused to celebrate when his team found the net, and he made Liverpool difficult to beat by building upon Houllier's defensive strength, adding compactness and positional discipline.

His debut season in charge witnessed Liverpool's first Champions League triumph in 21 years, after the Reds somehow defeated AC Milan after extra time and penalties despite being 3-0 down at the half-time interval. Liverpool's progression to the latter stages of the tournament and beyond captured the capricious nature of football as a sport. They didn't have the best players, finished fifth in the Premier League, but beat Chelsea – who were top that season – in the semi-finals by scoring a goal that famously didn't cross the line. What a sport. The power and atmosphere of Anfield had a significant impact on Liverpool's advancement throughout the tournament, and the character of the players is what sparked the comeback in Istanbul according to Benítez's own words, as opposed to any of his clever strategic moves.

Football doesn't always make sense. Perhaps that's why it's so popular as a global game, although Liverpool did benefit from doing their homework before the final took place. Speaking years later, Benítez explained how Liverpool conducted their own manual data collection exercise surrounding penalties. He said in an episode of *Monday Night Football* on Sky Sports:

> We had control of the penalties. When I was watching TV in Spain, I was taking notes of the penalties in Argentina, Brazil, any country, any game. I was taking notes and putting them in a computer database. Of the five Milan penalty takers, we didn't have the penalties for only Jon Dahl Tomasson. People said we were lucky but the year after we also won the FA Cup on penalties because we had the data.

It wasn't revolutionary, but considering it was 2005, it was a start.

Liverpool's cup heritage persisted under Benítez, and fresh investment from abroad allowed the club to compete with Manchester United and Chelsea for the Premier League title, or at least that was the plan. Tom Hicks and George Gillett brought Fernando Torres to Liverpool from Atlético Madrid in 2007. The deadly striker scored 65 Premier League goals in three and a half seasons under Benítez, and alongside Steven Gerrard became the heart of Liverpool's attack. The duo were telepathic at times. Everything associated with posing an offensive threat revolved around Torres, and his purchase was an unquestionable success, but the positivity surrounding Hicks and Gillett didn't stretch much further. The pair became known as cowboys who almost forced Liverpool into being repossessed by the banks.

Hicks began investing in sport in 1995 by purchasing the Dallas Stars, a professional ice hockey team. He also bought the Texas Rangers from none other than former American president George W. Bush in 1998, entering the Major League Baseball (MLB) world that John Henry would later conquer with the Boston Red Sox. Shortly after his baseball adventure began, Hicks personally negotiated the biggest contract in MLB history at that time, signing Alex Rodriguez on a ten-year contract. The deal would later hamper the success of the Rangers by restricting their efforts to sign other players, due to the funds tied up in Rodriguez's signature. Think along the lines of Antoine Griezmann to Barcelona in 2019. There are subtle differences, of course, but the Frenchman joined the Catalan club for over £100m, before getting loaned back to his previous club just two years later as Barcelona scrambled to clean up their financial mess. Lionel Messi, the club's greatest-ever player, was consequently forced to leave in the summer of 2021 because Barcelona simply couldn't afford to keep him.

One year after Hicks's baseball beginning, the Texan delved into the realms of football through his private equity firm and bought Cruzeiro and Corinthians, two of Brazil's leading clubs. His firm, Hicks, Muse, Tate and Furst, planned to start a South American cable sports channel to compete with ESPN, but four years later promises of a new stadium went unfulfilled by Hicks and his fellow stakeholders, and he left the group due to legal and financial troubles, paired with conflict between partners. Once Hicks came to England, Liverpool's plans for a new home followed a similar path, although Gillett was the bigger force behind acquiring the club. Unlike Hicks, who was more of an outsider, Gillett had a closer relationship with David Moores, the club's majority shareholder, and he had stalked the Premier League for some time. Throughout the years leading up to his arrival on Merseyside, Gillett had invested in NASCAR, ice hockey, American football and basketball, having once owned the famed Harlem Globetrotters. Across the board, Hicks and Gillett shared similarities. Each seemed to have somewhat of a scattergun approach to business dealings. As individuals their investments ranged from ski resorts to TV stations to soft drinks to marine transportation and everything in between.

Liverpool offered a fresh opportunity for the pair to get involved with football in Europe, but it didn't take long for their relationship to sour. Hicks and Gillett disagreed on several decisions, particularly those relating to stadium planning and Benítez remaining in charge of the team. At one stage Hicks attended a private meeting with Jürgen Klinsmann without Gillett in an attempt to source a potential successor to Benítez. Gerrard and Carragher were even quietly consulted about the decision, with Hicks effectively wanting the pair to give him the green light on behalf of the squad. 'I knew George Gillett from previous business deals that we'd ventured into together, where my firm owned 85 per cent compared to his 15 per cent, and he was impossible to deal with,' said Hicks when speaking to Sky Sports years later. Benítez was hindered by the club's owners, but he did manage to reach another Champions League Final in 2007, as well as finishing second in the Premier League in 2008/09.

'For five years, I had been a football manager at Liverpool,' Benítez later wrote in his book, *Champions League Dreams*. 'By the start of my sixth, it was clear I had become something else entirely. I was suddenly supposed to be a bank manager.' Navigating the transfer market was described as 'almost impossible' under Hicks and Gillett, who refused Benítez the funds to sign Fiorentina's Stevan Jovetić, and one of Portsmouth's Sylvain Distin or West Ham United's Matthew Upson in the summer after Liverpool finished second in the table. Whether any of those players would have improved the club's title aspirations remains to be seen. 'Decisions were being made to appease the banks, not the fans,' wrote Benítez. Once the Spaniard's six-year tenure ended, he was replaced by Roy Hodgson rather than Klinsmann. It was a disaster.

Liverpool, without any analysis department or sporting director at this stage, had picked up on Fulham's relative success under Hodgson during the previous campaign, in which the underdog Cottagers managed to reach the final of the UEFA Cup. Fulham eliminated holders Shakhtar Donetsk and Juventus on their journey, and Hodgson was voted the LMA Manager of the Year in the months before his Liverpool appointment, but he lasted just six months at Anfield. Hodgson's pragmatic and diplomatic ways failed to properly represent the fearless nature of Liverpool as a club and as a city. His last trophy had been won nine years prior to his appointment, and he was too inclined to dampen expectations and settle for normality to convince supporters that greatness was a realistic possibility.

Hodgson's ability to organise a team had helped him deliver respectable results across his career, but his tendency to rely on the sheer imagination of his creative players in attack – rather than choreographing creative team moves with possession – often seemed to limit the ceiling of his work, particularly when he came up against opponents who were willing to settle for a point. In many ways he wasn't too dissimilar to Benítez. The difference was in the Spaniard's desire to reach the pinnacle of the sport, his more recent record of success, his work at Valencia translating to the requirements of the job on Merseyside, and his more modern adaptation of what balanced football should look like.

When Henry's interest in buying Liverpool from Hicks and Gillett first emerged, Hodgson was still in charge. Joe Januszewski, who was senior vice-president for the Red

Sox's corporate sales at the time, was a Reds supporter from across the Atlantic, and he wasn't enjoying following his favourite Premier League team. The American, who would later end up being employed by the Texas Rangers that Hicks once owned, was part of the FSG delegation that headed to Merseyside to push through the eventual takeover bid. One month earlier, Januszewski was the person who made Henry aware of the ownership situation at Anfield by sending him an email, referencing the size of Liverpool in the footballing world and noting the reduced price the club could potentially be sold for. It was the ultimate business opportunity for FSG to consider, who had already effectively completed their mission in baseball. Januszewski even offered to act as a tour guide through his desperation for Liverpool to be placed in good hands. Henry, in keeping with his past, was naturally interested in capitalising upon an inefficiency in the market. This was his chance to acquire a sleeping giant on the cheap.

Liverpool sat just a few places from the bottom of the Premier League table at the time, having experienced a dismal summer in the transfer market. In what was to be the final window of the Hicks and Gillett tenure, Liverpool made a series of dreadful investments. They bought a 30-year-old version of Christian Poulsen from Juventus, and Paul Konchesky, who was 29 years old, from Hodgson's former club, Fulham, two players who had already delivered the best showings of their respective careers. Brad Jones, Danny Wilson and Jonjo Shelvey also came through the door for nominal fees, alongside Raúl Meireles, who contributed more than all the previous five names combined, albeit still not that much. Joe Cole and Milan Jovanović followed on free transfers, aged 28 and 29, as Liverpool desperately tried to make the money raised from Javier Mascherano's £18m sale to Barcelona stretch across multiple areas of need. Everything was about plugging holes and temporary fixes. Players were sold for less than their true worth on the pitch. Little consideration was given towards tomorrow's health, and sporting expertise was seriously lacking. Players were signed based on their past performances rather than what they would produce in the future.

After a much-publicised court battle in late 2010, Hicks and Gillett were forced to sell to FSG due to debt and a deadline set by the Royal Bank of Scotland. Henry's firm had previously identified French club Marseille as a possible avenue into European football, before Liverpool became available for a reduced price. Henry had overseen sporting success in his homeland, but this was an entirely different challenge. He believed that his background in data and his awareness of how to construct a successful sporting institution could give Liverpool an edge, but unlike baseball, football was a fluid and volatile game that incorporated far more than set-pieces on repeat. Basketball had a similar flowing nature to football, but it wasn't anywhere near as low-scoring. Liverpool's epic Champions League win in 2005 was evidence that football actively fought against logic. Would it be possible to decode such an ever-changing and random game using numbers, and could football really be solved?

Chapter Four

1,102 Ways to Get Worse

SPEAKING IN 2020, Peter Krawietz, Jürgen Klopp's long-term assistant, said, 'You can never lose, you can only learn,' to which Klopp replied, 'Defeat is only a waste of time if you don't learn from it. If you do, it can be the most important game of the whole season.' The comments were made in reference to losing a specific match, but they can also be applied to life and sport as a whole. Mistakes force us to explore alternatives. They make us wiser by teaching us about what doesn't work. They stimulate creativity.

Upon John Henry's takeover of Liverpool in 2010, he admitted to knowing 'virtually nothing' about Liverpool and the Premier League. He was clued up about sports, data and finance, among other things, but knew 'very little' about the world he was entering, according to his own words. FSG had aspirations to import their American model for success to England, but blunders seemed inevitable. Football, especially in England, was reluctant to change, particularly data, and that was going to remain the case until new ideas managed to deliver silverware, like Manchester United and their impact on Prozone in 1999.

FSG appreciated the value of employing a figure who governed the footballing side of the club from the summit; it ranked near the top of their initial to-do list. They wanted a Scouse version of Theo Epstein, in essence. The age-old manager was outdated. How could one individual be expected to dedicate enough time to adequately manage the squad, deliver coaching sessions, study opponents, scout for players from across the globe, employ members of staff, handle contract negotiations, promote talented players from within the youth ranks, and everything else, all at once? 'They want a management structure in place which they can identify with, from American or European models and not necessarily an archetypal English model,' said Roy Hodgson, who remained in charge of the team. Whether the person was to be labelled as a general manager, director of football, technical director, football director, sporting director or something even more exclusive, FSG recognised the value of creating the role based on their success in the US and appointed Damien Comolli less than one month after their Liverpool takeover was completed. Considering the importance of the position, FSG found their man pretty quickly, but the process was accelerated by the advice of one of Henry's old friends.

Comolli was recommended by Billy Beane after the pair formed a friendship on the back of the release of *Moneyball*. The Frenchman read the book before it was transformed for the big screen, and he was keen to reach out to Beane, meeting up with him on several occasions at sports conferences in the US and at the 2006 World Cup in Germany. The school of thought within *Moneyball* struck a chord with Comolli, who had been to watch the Oakland

Athletics as a teenager after his mother had been relocated to California for work purposes. He resonated with the story and began to adopt vaguely comparable methods in 2005 by becoming one of the very first in football to use data as part of his player evaluation process. 'Billy had been closely studying the Premier League,' said Henry. 'He called me shortly after the acquisition to recommend someone who had a similar viewpoint to his way of approaching baseball.'

Comolli was portrayed as one of the few data-driven thinkers in football at the time. He first came to England 14 years earlier as a European scout for the visionary Arsène Wenger, who had also worked with him at AS Monaco. For seven years, Comolli helped Arsenal identify prospects without numbers – from France in particular – including the likes of Kolo Touré, Emmanuel Eboué and Gaël Clichy. When his time as a scout ended, he stepped up to occupy a more senior position by becoming a sporting director at Saint-Étienne, before assuming an equivalent role at Tottenham Hotspur.

Daniel Levy brought Comolli to White Hart Lane. He was the chairman of the club and, like Henry, he knew the importance of placing responsibility on the shoulders of a central pillar who would hold everything together above the manager. In a conversation with *The Times* about the logic behind appointing a person upstairs, Levy said, 'The English manager comes in and wants to get rid of half of the players and bring in his own. So the club writes off millions by selling at a loss and buying all over again.' Wenger and Alex Ferguson, each of whom delivered success at Arsenal and Manchester United for over 20 years, conflicted with the new concept, having operated without a figure above them, but those two were rare exceptions, not examples. Comolli was tasked with disrupting the established order in the Premier League. In fact, the overall goal of his role at Spurs wasn't too dissimilar to Beane's objective in charge of the As. Comolli needed to pave a new way, it wasn't enough for him to follow the same route as his richer competitors. He naturally leaned on his new friend, who had all but completed the same assignment in MLB by using data and offbeat thinking to gain an edge over wealthier opponents.

On the back of *Moneyball*, Beane's contact list had become inflated, packed full of professionals across different sports who wished to share ideas while hoping to gain their very own version of an upper hand. Comolli pursued access to his expanding network and he eventually acquired the name of a person who could potentially help Spurs in Henry Stott, co-founder and managing director of a company called Decision Technology, now known as Dectech. The London-based organisation was originally founded to assess consumer behaviour across different industries, providing forecasts and predictions using data modelling. Football wasn't part of the plan until Stott attempted to use numbers to create an unpolished team strength model ahead of the 2002 World Cup, despite his lack of interest in the sport. He didn't support a club, recognised very few players and made the surprise move to suggest that Senegal were being underestimated as outsiders, and that in their first group match of the tournament against France – one of the favourites to win the competition – they had a reasonable 25 per cent chance of securing an upset. Indeed, Thierry Henry, Zinedine

Zidane and the rest of their elite team-mates lost by one goal to nil against El Hadji Diouf and Salif Diao, both of whom later ended up at Anfield, with Stott's firm consequently teaming up with Daniel Finkelstein at *The Times* to add a new layer to their football coverage, even beyond the World Cup.

The eventual product was the Fink Tank, a column that attempted to answer popular football questions in a humorous and light-hearted manner using data and legitimate evidence, rather than folklore and clichés. It was an attempt to debunk popular myths using facts and figures. Finkelstein and Decision Technology combined to evaluate whether a 2-0 lead was actually the most dangerous score in football. The Fink Tank, which Beane read on a regular basis, exposed whether long passes were more effective than short passes, whether smaller clubs did in fact raise their game to face heavyweight opposition, and whether playing at home is really an advantage or not, among other curious topics. It was through Finkelstein that Beane became aware of Stott, and it was through Beane that Stott was introduced to Comolli. After a meeting was arranged at the Spurs training ground in 2006, it was agreed that Decision Technology would provide consultancy services for the club. Comolli's initial proposal encouraged buying the company outright, but Levy, consistent with his unforgiving ways as an inflexible negotiator, was satisfied with striking an exclusive partnership instead.

Spurs signed many players, with Comolli overseeing their transfer operations, including Aaron Lennon, Tom Huddlestone, Dimitar Berbatov, Benoît Assou-Ekotto and Rafael van der Vaart. Decision Technology regarded the latter as undervalued in 2010, and suggested him as a suitable target for Comolli ahead of Ryan Babel, a tricky but relatively inconsistent forward who was liked by Harry Redknapp but had been starved of the necessary freedom that he required to prosper under Rafael Benítez at Anfield. The industrious and honourable qualities of Dirk Kuyt were preferred by the Liverpool boss, who shuddered at the thought of Babel attempting to substitute diligence for inventiveness without permission. Comolli sided with the advice provided to him by Decision Technology and sanctioned a deal to sign Van der Vaart from Real Madrid, and one of his Spurs signings travelled in the opposite direction for a world-record fee three years later.

Data wasn't wholly responsible for Comolli's capture of a 17-year-old Gareth Bale from Southampton in 2007, although he did curiously suggest that numbers were behind his usage as an attacker rather than a defender. Speaking to Irish radio station Newstalk, he said, 'We used data in terms of team selection. Data was showing Bale would be an outstanding left-winger, when Spurs were playing him at left-back.' It was a bold claim, especially considering data is nothing but noise until it has been translated. The meanings extracted can differ depending on the person involved and their own interpretation. Comolli never clarified exactly what data points suggested that Bale should be used further forward – perhaps Decision Technology helped – but nobody would argue with the unimaginable results of the tactical shift. The Welshman proceeded to score 43 goals in the Premier League before his move to the Spanish capital, while registering 20 assists and winning the PFA Players' Player of the Year award on two separate occasions.

Comolli also brought in Luka Modrić from Dinamo Zagreb. The slight but technically flawless Croatian was another who would end up sporting the famous white strip of Madrid in Spain, although Clive Allen suggested that he appeared on Spurs' radar due to plain old passing accuracy. In his autobiography, Allen stated that Comolli deserved credit for sourcing Modrić. 'Luka met his criteria in never giving the ball away,' wrote Allen, who was part of the Spurs coaching team. Of all the data points available to analyse players, pass completion ranks among the most basic. It's the most vanilla of all data points in football. A player could theoretically complete 50 passes in one match with every one travelling backwards, but he would consequently post 100 per cent accuracy. If used as a means of assuming skill or quality in possession, it can be dangerous and misleading without plenty of context. The fine details surrounding Comolli's identification of Modrić are lacking but, as Allen suggested, at least he was embracing the help of data, and the numbers helped him secure a gem.

'Damien has a proven track record of identifying exciting young footballing talent and we are delighted that he has agreed to join Liverpool,' said Henry. 'We intend to be bold and innovative.' Comolli had landed a top job, but his employers would later come to find that one of his biggest strengths was his ability to talk and paint himself in a positive light. He does have several success stories behind him, but the number of player acquisitions that directly stemmed from his foresight has always been open for debate. Some have suggested that rather than posting countless transfer hits for two of London's biggest clubs in Arsenal and Spurs, Comolli was in fact mostly responsible for spotting Clichy and Assou-Ekotto, each of whom moved to England from France as youngsters before playing at a respectable level. There was Van der Vaart and Modrić, but did he deserve points for signing those players, or were Decision Technology in fact operating as the brains behind the Spurs operation? Comolli certainly deserved a pat on the back for something. In a sense, he was ahead of virtually all his peers at the time, and he seemed far more open to what was new and unknown than your classic football man.

On Merseyside he would be afforded the luxury of time to rebuild Liverpool's squad, bringing down the average age and reducing the wage bill by signing players based on what they would do in the future rather than what they had done in the past. FSG wanted youth, perhaps too much so. Comolli was tasked with steering Liverpool away from the policy of signing players who had been around the block, such as Joe Cole and Christian Poulsen. Instead, he would attempt to devise a system to pick his players similar to how Henry would pick his stocks, or at least that was the plan. Liverpool shared parallels with Spurs. They didn't quite have the financial power to compete for the world's best and most expensive players at the time, and were forced to think outside the box instead. With rival clubs in England only getting richer, Liverpool had to do something different.

To his credit, Comolli's first signing was about as successful as it gets. After leaving Spurs in 2008, he proceeded to bring a scout named Steve Hitchen to Merseyside with him. He joined in 2011 and, weeks later, Liverpool agreed a £22.7m deal for a striker by the name of Luis Suárez, who Hitchen had scouted extensively while at White Hart Lane. The Uruguayan was packed full of character flaws and was almost a footballing equivalent of Babe Ruth in that sense, but his numbers for Ajax were outstanding. In the season before his switch, Suárez scored 35 times in the Dutch Eredivisie – eight of which were penalties – while also registering a further 16 assists from 33 appearances as a 22-year-old star in the making. His ability to deliver meaningful returns appeared proven, although the Eredivisie had a reputation for nurturing prospects rather than acting as a destination for players in their prime.

Signing Suárez was still a risk, especially considering he had just finished serving a seven-match ban for biting PSV Eindhoven's Otman Bakkal on the shoulder. He was a maniac at times. Suárez seemed quiet and reserved when he wasn't playing football, but whenever he was on the pitch he changed. Think about the difference between Bruce Banner and the Hulk. Six months before his move to Anfield, Suárez was controversially sent off in Uruguay's World Cup quarter-final against Ghana. He deliberately handled the ball on the line to keep out Dominic Adiyiah's goal-bound header in the last minute, and Ghana missed their resulting penalty seconds later. Suárez celebrated without guilt or embarrassment on the sidelines, and his team went on to progress by winning the decisive penalty shootout afterwards. He was a cheat, but he didn't care. 'I didn't miss the penalty,' he said without any hint of remorse when questioned about the incident over a decade later.

'For Luis, I looked at the stats over the last three years, notably the number of games played, which is an important factor,' said Comolli. 'We turn enormously toward players who don't get injured. We also took into account the number of assists, his performances against big teams, against the smaller clubs, in the Champions League, and the difference between goals scored at home and away.' Availability was a trait Comolli valued that would continue to be prioritised by Liverpool's scouting department further down the line. His analysis of Suárez was accurate. The berserk striker played for Liverpool for three and a half seasons and, over that period, he missed zero matches due to injury but several because of suspensions and punishments. He was a virtuoso with the ball, but Liverpool frequently had to ignore his personal defects to get the best from him.

Comolli made a strong start with Suárez in the door, but a storm followed that had quite a dramatic impact on Liverpool's future transfer business and bolstered the argument that data-driven recruitment would never work in football. Fernando Torres, who arrived at the club under Hicks and Gillett, announced his desire to leave in the same mid-season window that Suárez was signed. Selling him wasn't as much of a disaster as many supporters thought at the time, but this one was certain to trigger fury from the outside. 'This is a very significant day for Chelsea, capturing one of the best players in the world with his peak years ahead of him,' said Blues chairman Bruce Buck, but the Spanish striker only managed to find the net once in the Premier League throughout the rest of that campaign. In fact, Torres seemed to suffer from a rapid decline at Stamford Bridge, with 20 goals in 110 appearances for Chelsea in England's top flight, averaging one every 340 minutes compared to his rate of one every 120 minutes for Liverpool.

Without Benítez and Steven Gerrard presenting him with a platform to shine as the main man, Torres looked like a shadow of his Anfield self, but Reds supporters weren't to know that when he was controversially sold. After less than six months in charge, FSG had to sanction the sale of their prized asset to cash-rich Chelsea. To save face and keep the fanbase onside, Liverpool needed to find a replacement for Torres over the course of one weekend before the closure of the winter transfer window. Comolli's solution, somehow, was Andy Carroll.

A whopping £35m of the £50m that Liverpool raised by selling Torres was invested in the throwback striker, who has since admitted that while in a helicopter travelling to Merseyside he had to google the names of his new teammates. 'I'd never watch football,' he later told Newcastle United's club website. 'I'd come in on the Friday or wake up on the Saturday morning, saying, "Who are we playing?" I was just completely oblivious to all the football that was going on.' Standing around 6ft 3in tall, Carroll was a proper British warrior with long, flowing hair. The Geordie striker was a monster when challenging for the ball in the air and he was developing a reputation for being a real handful, even for the coolest of defenders. Carroll was 21 years old, home-grown and had experienced a promising 18-month period in front of goal, but he was the wrong man. After a conference call with FSG and Kenny Dalglish – who had replaced Hodgson earlier that month – Comolli approved the transfer late in the window. Carroll's conversion rate with his head was reported as a data point of interest to Comolli, who was no longer being supported by the experts at Decision Technology and seemed to suffer from his own analysis as a result, but he later admitted to buying him after receiving a tip that Newcastle's chairman would entertain a sale just 24 hours before the window closed.

After investing so much of the budget into Carroll, Comolli was forced to construct an entire team around him in the summer window that followed his transfer. His high-profile signing would shape the first iteration of Liverpool under FSG. Craig Bellamy joined on a free transfer because his physical statistics suggested that he was a worker for the team, according to Comolli, with the amount of distance covered by a player often wrongly understood to imply hard work and commitment. In the early days of Prozone, players who didn't cover as much ground as their team-mates were criticised and almost shamed by their managers, who translated the data without context when, in reality, running more has never necessarily equalled trying harder. The majority of Liverpool's transfer kitty was spent on Stewart Downing and Jordan Henderson, each of whom was signed for premium prices from clubs inside the Premier League.

Comolli championed chances created as his favourite metric that summer, which wasn't much more advanced than passing accuracy, and highlighted a problem attached to the use of data back then. Metrics within the sport were still pretty standard, and the big analytics expansion hadn't happened yet, primarily because of technological limitations. Downing and Henderson ranked near the top of the division for presenting their team-mates at Aston Villa and Sunderland with opportunities to score, and Charlie Adam followed the pair to Anfield from nearby Blackpool. The Scottish midfielder had shown up equally well by the same creative numbers. Comolli had signed a group of players who seemed capable of feeding Carroll's aerial powers with crosses, set-pieces and chances to find the net, but he had failed to consider the intelligence behind such an ancient and tired means of attacking.

In 2012, Will Morgan, now a senior data scientist at StatsBomb, a sports data business that first operated as a football blog consisting of data-powered content, had a closer look at Liverpool's crossing obsession in the season that followed the additions of Downing, Henderson and Adam. Dalglish had installed a brand of football to maximise the skills of the imposing Carroll, and it involved his team accumulating the most crosses in the Premier League, 1,102, which was 84 more than any other team and 265 above the division average. In his analysis, Morgan found that Liverpool attempted a cross roughly every 14 passes in the attacking half of the pitch, with only Wolves, Stoke City and Sunderland hitting crosses more frequently. Crucially, Liverpool averaged 421 open-play crosses per goal scored, which was the worst rate by a landslide and perhaps stemmed from Carroll not always being on the pitch due to minor injury problems. Wigan Athletic ranked as the next-worst outfit, scoring a goal every 294 crosses.

Ted Knutson, co-founder of StatsBomb, later wrote a data-driven summation, titled 'Things We Think We Know About Football – July 2013'. 'Crosses Are Bad' was his first subheading, and 'Headed Shots Are Bad' was his second. 'Strategies that revolve around crossing and heading are hugely inferior strategies,' Knutson wrote in his conclusion. Liverpool's tactical oversight was obvious. In another study, Garry Gelade, a sports analytics consultant who has worked with Chelsea, Real Madrid and Paris Saint-Germain, analysed some 33,954 crosses from three seasons of Premier League data. He found that only 666 were successful – a cross was deemed successful if it was followed by a goal within the next six seconds – which equated to just under two per cent.

Of course, not all crosses are the same. Deliveries can originate from different areas of the pitch, and they can be low, high, whipped or floated. With Dalglish at the helm – who hadn't managed a club in over a decade – Liverpool installed an obsolete approach that was more fashionable when he last assumed a role in football. His general idea was pure vintage. A nimble striker partnered a target man consisting of little more than brute force, and those two players were fed by natural wingers who simply ran towards the corner flag before hitting mostly aimless crosses towards the penalty spot. The intention was to be cutting edge, but Liverpool had gone back in time.

Having once been favoured as a primary attacking weapon by Ferguson's Manchester United at the top of the Premier League, crossing has suffered a consistent decline over the past decade. Back when Liverpool finished second under Benítez in 2008/09, the average Premier

League match consisted of around 35 open-play crosses. As the presence of data and the search for efficiency has evolved over time, that average has dropped to around 23 per match in today's game. It's still a prominent means of getting the ball into the penalty box, but unless the player who's delivering the crosses is David Beckham, football has realised that better decisions are often available to the player in possession.

FSG had ticked a few of the boxes on their checklist, but nothing was getting better. An unofficial mathematician was running Liverpool's transfer activity and data seemed to be informing his decisions in the market, but the Reds were getting worse. It was a steep learning curve, and Liverpool's struggles only provided more ammunition for the traditionalists who wished to berate the club for attempting to do things differently. Just 18 months after Carroll moved to Liverpool, he joined West Ham United on a six-month loan deal before being sold on a permanent basis for less than half of the amount he was bought for.

Around ten years down the line, Comolli was appointed as president of Toulouse, and he made the curious decision to install what he described as a 'truth teller' by his side. 'During my career as a director, the biggest mistakes I made happened when I was isolated,' he told the *Training Ground Guru* podcast. Carroll was a tragic but necessary error. His fruitless transfer exemplified a bunch of teachings for Liverpool to learn from and enforce in the future. Buying nobody can prove to be a healthier long-term move than buying the wrong player in some cases. It can take several windows to recover from signing the wrong player. Transfers guided by agent recommendations rather than internal analysis can be perilous. Gathering information about the person behind the player is imperative. Panic buying out of desperation tends to result in overpaying. The risk attached to buying a player has to be minimised, and it has to be worth the potential reward. Some footballing strategies are less optimal than others. If your data suggests that Charlie Adam is the answer, reconsider.

Chapter Five

The Art of Dying

LIVERPOOL SUPPORTERS expect to witness victories when visiting Anfield. Regardless of the opposition, anything less than a win is typically deemed as a disappointment, yet in 2011 the stadium broke into applause after the final whistle of a lifeless 0-0 draw. Spectators appreciated and admired what they had observed, only the pleasant reception wasn't directed at Liverpool, it was aimed at their opponents. As Kenny Dalglish continued to conduct Liverpool's flawed crossing experiment, a team visited Merseyside and advocated their own approach. The group of players underlined possession-based football and wished to build flowing moves from one end of the pitch to the other, with the ball glued to the floor at all times. It was imperative for their passes to remain grounded, especially considering their midfield consisted of three players standing 5ft 4in, 5ft 6in and 5ft 10in tall. Liverpool hadn't faced Barcelona. They hadn't faced Ajax or Arsenal, either. Their opponents on the day were Swansea City, who had been promoted from the Championship just six months earlier. The majority of the players who featured in the match will probably remember the date. 'Write that down in your diary,' said Brendan Rodgers after the bout. '5 November 2011, you got a standing ovation from the Anfield crowd.'

Swansea's underdog performance against Liverpool wasn't just a flash in the pan. By the end of the campaign, Rodgers had guided the Welsh outfit to 11th in the Premier League table. They had finished just five points behind Liverpool despite spending around 20 per cent as much on new signings in the previous summer transfer window. Their final standing was praised, but it was the way in which they attained their results that created a stir. Swansea ended the season with 20,795 passes to their name, which placed them behind only Manchester City in the Premier League, who were crowned as champions. Arsenal ranked third on 20,613 and Liverpool placed as low as sixth, some 1,998 passes behind Swansea. Like many of the most celebrated coaches throughout the history of the sport, Rodgers had managed to get his players to advertise the type of football that he cherished. For a man who names José Mourinho as his single biggest managerial influence, his stylistic preferences couldn't have been further from those of his mentor.

His brand of football was as much about what he wanted to see as it was about what he required during his own days as a player. Standing just 5ft 7in tall, injuries prevented Rodgers from having a full professional career, but before his premature retirement as a 20-year-old prodigy, he felt in conflict with the nuts and bolts of British football. 'The culture was very long and direct and that didn't suit me as a player,' he told the FA when asked about his philosophy. 'I was a technician, but the game I was asked to play wasn't really how I enjoyed playing.' Rodgers knew how to talk up his own skills, it was a strength of his. He could make Damien Comolli sound relatively modest. 'My football philosophy is very much about positive football,' said Rodgers. 'If you want to define it: we like to play attacking and creative football, but always with a tactical discipline. The template for all of our work is our organisation.' Armed with all of the necessary buzzwords to sell his vision, Rodgers seemed ahead of the curve. He had continental methods, and wanted to prove their credentials in the muddy fields of England. Rodgers was all about believing in a fixed identity rather than making wholesale strategic adjustments from match to match. His team were even nicknamed 'Swansalona' at one stage, with light-hearted comparisons made to Pep Guardiola's all-encompassing Barcelona.

During his primordial years as a coach, Rodgers was sacked after just 23 matches in charge of Reading. Shane Long played under him during the spell and later recalled his struggles. 'You can see how Swansea play attractive football, but it just didn't seem to work at Reading,' he said. 'Passing football, extra bodies in midfield, passing it around opponents. The Barcelona way of playing, more or less.'

It was natural for Rodgers to seek inspiration from Guardiola. In fact, he might have been a little too inspired by him at one stage, having made the curious decision to start speaking Spanish during a team meeting while in charge of the Royals. There wasn't a single Spanish player in the room at the time. Guardiola was the master of coaching his players to keep the element of chance under wraps. He was an enhanced and more intense version of Arsène Wenger in many ways, and had been nurtured from a young age in the classrooms of Barcelona's celebrated academy, La Masia. Possession was everything to him. 'I like the ball, I love the ball,' he said. 'To score a goal, you need the ball. As long as you have it and your percentage is higher, you have more of a chance of scoring a goal.' The fundamental idea behind Guardiola's philosophy was incredibly simple, yet it seemed to be wholly neglected in England, with Charles Reep sitting at the complete opposite end of the scale. In his first stint in charge of a senior team at Barcelona, Guardiola won 14 major honours in four seasons – including two Champions League titles – albeit with the best player in the history of the sport at his disposal.

British coaches mostly tended to downplay the importance of establishing control with the ball like Guardiola, but Rodgers separated himself from the pack. 'I enjoy winning, but I like to control how to win,' he said. 'I liked Dutch and Spanish football principles and how they could control games. I visited Barcelona, Valencia and Sevilla to gain experience and broaden my coaching horizons.' Rodgers didn't have a background in numbers, but he subconsciously seemed to hold an interest in probability. The stereotypically time-worn British manager prioritised the defensive side of the game, and relied upon the genius of one or two individuals to deliver goals at the opposite end. It was a widely accepted practice, but it wasn't a sustainable means of accumulating attacking returns and winning matches. In terms of having some form of control over the unpredictable sport that was football, Rodgers had the right idea, although his beliefs originated from a utopian perspective on the game rather than any faith in science or mathematics. 'The British type of football was very much about smashing it up the pitch and playing the percentages,' he said. 'The only percentage I was interested in was possession and I didn't think it was rocket science. If we have the ball, you can't score, no matter how big or strong you are. I've always worked off that.'

During his relatively short spell in Wales, Rodgers demonstrated an ability to make his team more than the sum of its parts. His players, for the most part, weren't of the required standard to compete in the Premier League. As individuals they were pretty average. Through modern coaching, effective man-management and the foundation of a common tactical idea, Rodgers seemed to showcase a rare quality in the managerial world by having an actual impact on his team's performances. Swansea finished 11th in the table, but it wasn't a fluke.

Assessing managerial performance can be a difficult task. 'This is a game where the coach has less margin than any coach in another sport. This is a continuous sport in which the coach has barely any influence,' Ernesto Valverde, formerly of Barcelona, told the *Financial Times* in 2019. 'We only have three substitutions, the game never stops. Football belongs to the players. For 45 minutes at a time, the player makes his own decisions.' The Spaniard's words capture some of the issues attached to evaluating managers in football. How does one go about distinguishing how much of a team's success or failure should be attributed to the manager in comparison to the players on the pitch?

It's a matter that was tackled by the Fink Tank on more than one occasion, with the help of Decision Technology. Henry Stott paired with Ian Graham, one of his statisticians – who would later become a prominent figure on Merseyside – to make sense of the chaotic world of management in 2005, and they delivered their insights to Daniel Finkelstein, who wrote the column. 'On average, managers arrive and leave without having significantly altered the team strength. The board has gone to a whole load of trouble for nothing,' he wrote in his conclusion.

Stott and Graham teamed up three years later with a new colleague in Mark Latham to explore the topic once more. Harry Redknapp, who had been appointed by Tottenham Hotspur – clients of Decision Technology – just a month earlier, was regarded as a difference-making boss in their analysis based on his first stint in charge of Portsmouth. Overall, though, a large percentage of managers seemed to follow the same pattern, benefiting from an initial bounce after being appointed, which often degrades over time, resulting in a period of stagnation before a decline and a sacking.

Speaking to the *New York Times* in 2023, Graham briefly revisited the topic, stating that assessing the power of managers was the 'holy grail' of analytics. 'That's very complicated,' he said. 'It tends to be conflated with who has the best players, the best team. There are a lot of second-order effects. It's very hard to know exactly how good any manager is, and what sort of impact they have on results.' Few appear to make a worthwhile difference, with most proving to be neither positive nor negative, but Rodgers looked like enough of an outlier who was worth exploring.

Liverpool persevered with crossing 30 times per match for just one season, before Dalglish was sacked after finishing eighth in the table. The Reds legend had delivered the League Cup while also reaching the final of the FA Cup against Chelsea – losing by two goals to one – but his relative success in knockout tournaments had masked the fact that Liverpool were essentially going nowhere under his leadership in terms of a gradual evolution towards what FSG had intended. Supporters in England tend to go crazy when managers are sacked immediately after winning trophies, but the football played at Anfield was primordial, with a renovation job very much in order. Dalglish was an obvious fan-favourite on Merseyside and that likely wouldn't have changed even if he had lost every single match in charge, but it was the right decision to install fresh ideas.

Liverpool's eighth position in the table that season remains the club's joint-lowest finish of the Premier League era. Rodgers, armed with a 180-page dossier that detailed the intricacies of his polished philosophy, was installed as the team's new boss ahead of Roberto Martínez, who had established a comparable possession-based style at Wigan Athletic and also seemed to have an impact on team performance. Liverpool's tactical design had changed. Old-fashioned crossing didn't work, the ball had to be cared for. Rodgers would be the figure to teach the players how to govern proceedings in a sustainable way, but his appetite for control trickled into off-pitch matters.

Unlike Hodgson and Dalglish, Rodgers was adamant that he wouldn't work with a sporting director. In fact, he claimed to have turned down the Liverpool job three times before clarifying his status as the club's ringleader. Comolli had been sacked one month earlier, to his surprise but nobody else's. The owners weren't convinced by his investments, and labelled him as responsible for shaping the club's fresh start around Andy Carroll's supernatural heading ability. FSG wanted to replace Comolli and stick with their prearranged management structure, until Rodgers and his charming powers of persuasion convinced them to make a more significant change.

'They are still learning the game,' said Rodgers about his new employers, without any hint of condescension. 'I am better when I have control. I am not a power freak. If you are the manager of the club and someone else tells you to have that player, it doesn't work.' His words should have raised a red flag for FSG, but Rodgers had a magnetism about him. He was a skilled wordsmith, capable of selling Christmas trees in January. In addition to failing to grasp the true concept of a model that incorporated a sporting director, Rodgers had provided FSG with a glimpse into his egotistical character by refusing to work under a person upstairs. *Being: Liverpool*, a fly-on-the-wall series that covered his first season at Anfield, offered further evidence into his curious nature. In one of the six episodes, cameras filmed on Merseyside and captured footage of an enormous portrait of Rodgers hanging in the lounge of his own home, which would later be occupied by Jürgen Klopp. The piece of art was actually a gift from a disabled charity in Wales but, at the time, no context was added surrounding the scene, and it didn't paint Rodgers in the best light.

Over the course of his managerial career, his name would become quietly associated with that of David Brent, the famous fictional star of *The Office*, who was known for his comedic approach to the management of a paper merchant in Slough. 'My biggest mentor is myself because I've had to study, so that's been my biggest influence.' That was Rodgers, not Brent. He was a know-it-all at heart, and his make-up seemed destined to conflict with FSG's overall ambition to construct a collaborative data-charged club. Rodgers would eventually have to listen to those who seemed less qualified than himself to talk about football.

He would eventually have to buy into the intelligence of others as opposed to setting his own judgement in stone, but despite his blemishes, he did seem to know the score in a philosophical sense.

'We have recruited a young and exciting manager who will bring a style of attacking, relentless football,' said Tom Werner after appointing Rodgers. His first Premier League match at the helm was against West Bromwich Albion. Liverpool lost 3-0, seeing 60 per cent of the ball despite going down to ten men in the 58th minute, with Daniel Agger receiving a red card. For all the excitement around the club's new direction, Rodgers needed six Premier League matches to secure his first win. The overemphasis on possession seemed to have a negative impact on the players at the beginning of his tenure. Everything was about style; substance was less important. Liverpool were lured towards the classic booby trap of playing in order to dominate possession, rather than playing in order to win matches through the use of it. Possession has to have life and purpose, otherwise it's meaningless, but those lines can often become tangled.

A full season of mediocrity passed before things improved. Liverpool finished seventh under Rodgers in his debut campaign, but one year later they almost won the Premier League as rookie outsiders. Several players signed under Comolli's watch began to show their worth in 2013/14, most notably Luis Suárez, Daniel Sturridge and Jordan Henderson. The Uruguayan was the real hotshot under Rodgers. Suárez missed the first five matches of the Premier League season for biting Chelsea's Branislav Ivanović months earlier, yet he still managed to equal Cristiano Ronaldo's record for the most goals scored in a single 38-match campaign at the time. He found the net on 31 occasions – without taking a single penalty – while also registering 12 assists. Suárez was directly responsible for around 43 per cent of Liverpool's remarkable total of 101 goals, with Sturridge contributing 29 per cent. Suárez's output in the Netherlands had seemingly translated into English football.

Henderson was reported as one of the reasons behind Comolli's sacking, but under Rodgers he thrived as an energetic box-to-box midfielder who could run forever. 'The day I got sacked, [FSG] told me I had made a big mistake on Jordan and he was a waste of money,' Comolli told talkSPORT. Signed as a 20-year-old starlet, Henderson was picked up due to the number of chances he seemed to create while playing for a lesser club. He was another means of feeding Carroll in Comolli's eyes, but although he did prove to be a huge success for the club further down the line, he didn't prosper because of his invention on the ball. Comolli now views Henderson as another one of his transfer wins, but his initial reason behind signing him didn't exactly correlate with the player he later became. Rodgers used him as an engine instead of a creator. Henderson was the ultimate team player who thrived when presented with a functional role. Rodgers harnessed his capacity to cover the ground of two men by encouraging him to do the running for an ageing Steven Gerrard, who was often fielded behind him, with forwards Philippe Coutinho and Raheem Sterling also benefiting from his industrious presence. Comolli later claimed that Henderson showed up as a physical monster in the numbers, thanks to data provided by Prozone. 'We knew his physical abilities, his fitness stats were absolutely unbelievable,' he said in an attempt to cleanse his troublesome tenure on Merseyside.

Suárez and Sturridge in particular exploded in that 2013/14 season. They offered the substance that was lacking beforehand, but despite Liverpool's sudden resurgence as an elite offensive unit, the control that Rodgers had always talked about was nowhere to be found. His players guaranteed goals, but they had very little command over proceedings on the pitch and struggled to relax the tempo when necessary. Liverpool scored over a century of goals, but conceded exactly half a century on the defensive side of the game. Manchester City, who finished top of the Premier League, shipped 13 fewer goals in comparison, with as many as seven teams conceding fewer than Liverpool. Hull City, who finished 16th, conceded 53 times.

'I like to control how to win,' said Rodgers, but his very best team at Anfield was rapid, direct and haphazard. Liverpool won matches in ferocious 20-minute spells. They didn't play like Swansea or Guardiola's Barcelona. In fact, Liverpool finished the season over 1,500 passes behind the Swans once again, who had appointed Danish legend Michael Laudrup to replace Rodgers. Liverpool wanted to exchange punches and had the necessary talent in offensive areas to win by trading blows. They scored at least three goals in 21 of their 38 matches but, as a consequence of their eagerness to accelerate the game whenever possible, they allowed too much at the opposite end.

Rodgers was certainly an offensive-minded coach, but throughout his three-and-a-half year stay at Anfield, Liverpool never had that much control over their own destiny. He's a self-proclaimed possession-based coach who doesn't always view possession as the best means of posing a threat and winning matches. Swansea had demonstrated a clear intent to keep the ball, and Celtic were equally dominant during his two and a half years in Scotland, but while in charge of Liverpool, and Leicester City years later, Rodgers placed more of an emphasis on harnessing the qualities of his speedy attackers by making use of forward passes and quick attacks. In every one of his jobs since Reading, it could be argued that his ability to make his team more than the sum of its parts has largely persisted. He does seem to be a manager who has an individual impact on team strength, particularly around 12 to 24 months into his tenure, but his approach is perhaps more muddled than he thinks. Unlike Guardiola, who has obsessed over possession at every one of his clubs, Rodgers has compromised the crux of his philosophy to secure results on numerous occasions. He's almost evolved into more of a strategist than a philosopher as he's gained experience at the highest level, although he would probably argue otherwise.

By the end of his time at Anfield, Liverpool had lost all sense of identity. Rodgers had morphed into a weird mixture of different people, almost forgetting who he was in the process. He talked about passing and control when he first arrived. Then his players thrived by playing in a quick and direct manner. Then he announced his intention to take his team in a new 'technical direction' as he scrambled to save his job after a 6-1 loss to Stoke City in the final match of Liverpool's 2014/15 season, agitating for the signature of giant Christian Benteke from Aston Villa. Rodgers didn't deliver a single piece of silverware during his time on Merseyside, but his appointment was a step in the right direction for FSG and, for a short period, his players offered a glance into the future, performing as an aggressive unit who imposed their speed and liveliness upon proceedings, while thriving as a collective.

In the summer of 2014, Liverpool were playing their football in sunny Miami. They were taking part in a pre-season tournament alongside the likes of Manchester United, Manchester City and Olympiacos. The new Premier League campaign was scheduled to start in two weeks' time as Liverpool faced AC Milan in a friendly, winning by two goals to nil. Nobody could have foreseen the two clubs doing business for a high-maintenance outcast just 22 days later.

Rodgers had just lost the player who he'd constructed his attack around. Liverpool's talisman, Suárez, had been sold to Barcelona for a fee thought to be in the region of £75m. He was the player who set the tone for everything at Anfield. In one fell swoop, Rodgers lost almost half of his team's Premier League goals from the previous season, yet nobody panicked. In fact, everybody took a holiday. Suárez's departure didn't matter, Liverpool were back. Only Manchester City had finished above them in the previous season. The dark days were thought to be over, but another storm was coming. Rodgers had banked on landing Alexis Sánchez, who seemed to be a ready-made replacement for Suárez, from Barcelona in the same transfer window, but the Chilean forward decided to join Arsenal instead. The Northern Irishman didn't have as much pull as he thought at Anfield, with Wenger described as one of the reasons behind Sánchez's decision to choose London over Merseyside.

As the new season commenced, the reality of failing to identify an alternative option to Sánchez began to hit home, and as the window approached its closure, Liverpool agreed a shock £16m deal for Mario Balotelli. 'I can categorically tell you Mario Balotelli will not be at Liverpool,' said Rodgers after beating Milan weeks earlier in Florida. There was a reason Rodgers was so stern with his statement. Balotelli was a complete enigma. From throwing darts at youth players, to setting his own house alight with fireworks, to handing out £50 notes to strangers in the streets of Manchester, stories about his off-pitch antics had become part of football folklore. In spite of all his potential, the Italian striker simply lacked interest. He didn't care. Mourinho once described him as 'unmanageable', yet he had somehow ended up as a replacement for one of the world's most influential players. Liverpool had found a person who was even more bewildering than Suárez, but one who was nowhere near as competitive as him once he assumed the form of a player on the pitch. Within four months of coaching him, Rodgers publicly claimed that pressing and intensity wasn't part of Balotelli's game, despite those two staples proving to be central to Liverpool's previous make-up with Suárez.

Every man and his dog had an opinion on how Liverpool should have replaced their star man that summer. The data wizards at StatsBomb wrote a piece on the topic at the time, and their search for players who were statistically similar to Suárez returned two unrealistic names: Arjen Robben and Lionel Messi. Once delving a little deeper, StatsBomb recommended Xherdan Shaqiri, who would end up joining Liverpool four years later, and Memphis Depay as players who seemed to be capable of leading an attacking department almost single-handedly by creating chances for themselves and others.

Prozone also conducted an exercise to replace Suárez in one of their Performance.LAB seminars. They identified that Liverpool had essentially stopped using quick and direct attacks with Balotelli in Suárez's place, having previously operated as one of the keenest counter-attacking units in the Premier League, and used data to hone in on addressing that particular detail. After removing Messi, Cristiano Ronaldo and Sergio Agüero from their search, players such as Ciro Immobile, Kevin Gameiro, Robert Lewandowski, Domenico Berardi, Carlos Tevez and Diego Costa, who Liverpool tried to sign from Atlético Madrid 12 months earlier, showed up as suitable candidates, assuming Rodgers wanted to recover his team's counter-attacking strength. Prozone used goals per 90 minutes and counter-attacking distance covered per 90 minutes to narrow down their search. The study was relatively foundational, but it offered an insight into how player recruitment in football was changing. A longlist of players could be condensed in a very short space of time. Metrics were becoming increasingly advanced and, providing they were used correctly, they had the power to make scouting easier and considerably more efficient.

Rodgers lost his identity at Anfield, but for all his vague stylistic changes and curious tactical decisions, recruitment was the main source of his undoing, and the club's summer transfer window in 2014 epitomised everything that was wrong with Liverpool's practices. When Rodgers refused to work under a sporting director upon his appointment, he unconsciously proclaimed that he didn't need help. 'I always think the manager is the technical director,' he said. He knew all about the players who suited his brand of football, and he was allowed to bring several of them to Anfield. By the time the infamous summer window of 2014 had rolled around, Joe Allen and Fabio Borini were already at the club after being specifically recommended by Rodgers. Adam Lallana followed for around £25m, even though the scouts and the scientists at the club had doubts about him. Rodgers knew what he wanted. 'I like players who can deal with the ball, who are technically strong,' he said. 'I like players who tactically understand the game and players who want to learn.' Over time, he developed a tendency for signing players who almost reflected his own limitations when he was a player. Rodgers became known for labelling his favourites as 'technicians', and he didn't seem to place much importance on physical qualities. The signature Rodgers player was lightweight and aesthetically pleasing on the eye, but simply didn't have much of an impact on results or goal difference.

Although Rodgers was granted his wish to work without a sporting director, he did have to collaborate as part of a so-called 'transfer committee' at Liverpool. The initial party consisted of Rodgers, scouts Dave Fallows and Barry Hunter, head of analysis Michael Edwards, FSG's Anfield representative Mike Gordon and CEO Ian Ayre. The aim was for several minds to bond and exchange wisdom about potential transfers, but from an outside perspective the group seemed to converse like a dysfunctional family of siblings. To keep everybody satisfied, Liverpool purchased a mixed bag of players. Some were signed for Rodgers, whereas others were pushed by the rest of the committee. A move for Sturridge was given the green light by the scouts and the analysts, for example, but not by Rodgers, and the same goes for Roberto Firmino.

In 2014, Liverpool showed the world what the product of a transfer committee with two minds looked like. With the Suárez money burning a hole in the club's pocket, Liverpool splashed the cash on several new arrivals. Balotelli, Lallana, Lovren, Lazar Marković, Alberto Moreno, Divock Origi, Emre Can and Rickie Lambert joined for well over £100m. Lambert, who was the cheapest of the incomings and was 32 years old, was demanded by Rodgers due to how one specific match had cost his team the Premier League just months earlier. In his eyes, Liverpool didn't lose the title because of their lack of control or their shambolic defence throughout the campaign, they lost because of one isolated result.

Liverpool's hold over the summit of the Premier League loosened after the Reds lost to Mourinho's stubborn Chelsea outfit, who wasted time and refused to venture beyond their own defensive third from the first whistle. After Gerrard slipped and allowed Chelsea to gain an undeserved lead in the 48th minute, Liverpool banged their heads against a brick wall for the remainder of the bout. Desperate to atone for his error, Gerrard tried to save the result in typical Gerrard fashion by doing it all himself, attempting a countless number of sub-optimal shots from 25 yards out. Liverpool failed to break through Chelsea's roadblock, but rather than suggesting that his players should have remained patient by playing the extra pass, Rodgers seemed to think his team lost because of what they didn't possess on the bench.

Liverpool didn't have a Plan B, in his mind. The option of introducing a physical focal point – perhaps in the mould of a certain Andy Carroll – was lacking and it consumed Rodgers. The result wasn't necessarily his fault from his perspective, and the solution wasn't to improve Plan A through delicate enhancements on the training ground, it was to have a fallback if Plan A didn't work. Perhaps Rodgers was more British than he thought. Liverpool proceeded to chase Lambert and 12 months later also signed Benteke from Aston Villa for over £30m, despite the scouts and the analysts on Merseyside advising against his transfer. Benteke offered more than Lambert and Carroll in a tactical sense, but he still wasn't overly different to the quintessential target man. Rodgers was determined to protect himself from ever suffering due to the lack of a Plan B again. Romelu Lukaku's name was even suggested as a compromise by Edwards around the time of Benteke's signing, but his mind was made up. In the same summer window, Liverpool bought Firmino from Hoffenheim for around £29m after the Brazilian had shown up in the data as the best forward in Europe who was both affordable and attainable. The two deals were made just four weeks apart, and they illustrated the ongoing tug of war between Rodgers and the rest of the transfer committee. He wanted Benteke, his colleagues wanted Firmino, and the middle ground resulted in both moving to Merseyside. Little consideration seemed to be given towards how the duo would perform together, especially considering neither possessed enough natural speed and acceleration to threaten in behind defences.

Football is rife with red herrings. The sport has provided a countless number of examples of clubs blindly identifying the wrong areas to address in order to improve on the pitch. Media narratives that are spun based upon little more than raw opinion can gather traction, and they can send your club on a wild goose chase in search of what isn't actually required. Club A needs a striker, Club B needs to sack their head coach, Club C needs a Plan B, Club D needs a direct replacement for X, who has just been sold. The utopia that FSG imagined was never going to be reached with Rodgers as the captain of the ship. He's never publicly portrayed himself as a sceptic of data as such, but his stumbling block at Liverpool was his unwavering faith in his own judgement. Ego was king. For data to have a worthwhile impact on the direction of any organisation inside and outside of football, empowerment and endorsement is paramount. Those occupying power positions have to buy into new ideas, and alignment is essential. The world's best player is redundant if he remains on the bench, and the world's best data scientists are redundant if nobody listens to them. Rodgers was too opinionated to surrender to the expertise of others, and it resulted in his sacking.

Of all the voices heard in the committee, Rodgers clashed with Edwards the most. A former Prozone analyst who had previously headed up performance analysis departments at Portsmouth and Tottenham Hotspur, he first joined Liverpool in 2011. He was appointed to construct an analysis department from the ground up, having been headhunted by Damien Comolli, who had been introduced to him when the pair worked in tandem at Spurs. 'I liked the fact that he challenged conventional wisdom, like Billy Beane,' Comolli later told *The Independent*, still captivated by his *Moneyball* idol.

Aside from a short spell as a teenager at Peterborough United, Edwards didn't have much playing experience. He was effectively forced out of football and into life as an IT teacher at one stage, picking up a degree in business management and informatics at the University of Sheffield. Good fortune and a relationship with Redknapp is what brought him from Portsmouth to Spurs. The vintage English manager was traditional in his ways and he certainly wasn't inclined to place much weight on numbers and statistics, but he took a shine to Edwards and took him to White Hart Lane with him. A popular story about Redknapp placing a CD-ROM containing player data into the CD player of his car summed up his green understanding of newfangled methods, but that was why he valued Edwards. Having played as a footballer himself – albeit as a youngster – Edwards had a valuable skill set that was relatively scarce at the time. He could handle modern technology and interpret numbers in a practical footballing sense, but also possessed the necessary interpersonal skills to communicate his findings to players, coaches and dreaded 'football men'. He was capable of translating data before delivering succinct conclusions to the people who mattered most.

After Comolli brought him from London to Merseyside, his prominence steadily grew. Edwards was a bright and sharp mind, but despite his preference to drift under the radar and avoid the public spotlight, Rodgers viewed him as a threat to his authority. The two had differing perspectives on the concept of squad building, and Edwards was gradually assuming the form of the sporting director that Rodgers had vowed not to work with. Around 13 months after Rodgers was dismissed, Edwards was promoted by Gordon – once described by John Henry as FSG's 'most knowledgeable person with regard to soccer' – to become Liverpool's new technical director. An article in the *Daily Mail* characterised Edwards as 'the laptop guru who did a number on Brendan Rodgers'. He was knocked for having 'a lack of playing experience at any relevant level' and for spelling 'the end of the road for good football men' such as scouts who travelled up and down the country with little more than a notepad in hand to evaluate players. The parallels between Liverpool and Boston were becoming obvious. Traditional wisdom was being questioned by supposedly inexperienced apprentices who brought new ideas to the table, which resulted in resistance from seasoned figures. Edwards almost became Liverpool's take on Theo Epstein or Daryl Morey. He didn't fit the criteria according to the rule book, but that didn't matter.

In Edwards, FSG had finally placed a man who would consult and understand data at the forefront of their football operation. Further down the line, he would laugh off public suggestions that he was a 'stats man' in an open letter to Liverpool supporters after announcing his departure from the club in 2021. In an article by *The Athletic*, he was described as having a 'fetish for numbers and statistics' but, due to his undercover profile, his true interest in facts and figures remains largely concealed, and he wouldn't have it any other way.

Chapter Six

The Goldilocks Zone

FOOTBALL IS everything to coaches, players and supporters alike. The next match is all that matters. It's all or nothing, according to Amazon. 'Some people believe football is a matter of life and death,' Bill Shankly once said. 'I am very disappointed with that attitude. I can assure you it is much, much more important than that.' The footballing calendar runs in seasons rather than years. In England, all resources are dedicated towards delivering as much success as possible from August until May and, as a result, short-term thinking is an insidious problem. Decisions are made to plug holes, to survive and to get over the line. The repercussions aren't given a second thought until next season, or perhaps the season after, when the chickens come home to roost. The sport is painted as a finite game because winners and losers are decided at the end of every campaign. Like poker or bingo, the game appears to have an ending, but that isn't wholly accurate.

Football is an infinite game in a wider context. The sport never truly ends. Liverpool will continue to exist regardless of what happens at the end of the season.

Football, despite pivotal moments and all-important finals, is an ongoing experience, and in 2012 FSG instructed Damien Comolli to behave like that was the case. Months before the Frenchman was sacked from his role, FSG informed Comolli that he was only able to sign players who were under the age of 21. The budget per player was around £10m. Liverpool had bought too many ageing players who had struggled to add value, and it was time for a change. Comolli began to chase youthful players who could offer years of service while gradually increasing in value, and Billy Beane thought it made plenty of sense:

> You know why they sign younger players? The reason is because they are cost-effective. They may cost more to acquire, but their wages are lower. With an older player you may be paying for past performance, whereas with a younger player you are paying for future performance. It is like stock. Young players are attractive because they are cheaper and offer more value. They may not be as good, but if they perform at a certain level it makes more sense financially.

John Henry knew how to invest in stock, and signing younger players was a smart move, but this was Liverpool. Any patience would have to be coupled with some degree of urgency given the demand for success at Anfield. 'We're always tomorrow-based, we're always thinking about tomorrow,' said Henry, but in doing so Liverpool almost forgot to think about today. As Comolli prioritised potential rather than proven product, he brought a number of prospects to the club, including Philippe Coutinho, Oussama Assaidi, Samed Yeşil, Tiago Ilori, Luis Alberto and Iago Aspas.

The latter two ended up acting as curious case studies. Alberto arrived at the club for around £7m from Sevilla and, in the same week, Aspas joined from Celta Vigo for just under £10m. The Spaniards were still young at the time, one aged 20 and the other aged 25. They were both slight, slender and inexperienced, and they represented FSG's new transfer policy. In the season before he joined Liverpool, Alberto delivered 27 scoring returns in the currency of goals and assists while on loan at Barcelona B. He was an offensive midfielder and regarded as a rough diamond who seemed to fit the 'technician' profile that Brendan Rodgers liked. Aspas had experienced even greater success in his homeland. Across his previous two league campaigns, the striker had 49 scoring returns to his name, including just five penalties. He rarely missed a match and was deemed to be worth taking a gamble on.

Despite the promise surrounding the duo, neither prospered at Liverpool. Alberto made just nine Premier League appearances – all as a substitute – and Aspas accumulated only 14, with neither managing to score a single goal. Rodgers struggled for squad depth throughout his time in charge of Liverpool, particularly in 2013/14 with a Premier League title very much in sight, yet still proved to be reluctant to use Alberto and Aspas as extra bodies or impact substitutes. After being sold further down the line, the two players would go on to have successful careers. Alberto joined Lazio in Italy and Aspas rejoined his former club, Celta Vigo. Across the four seasons between 2017 and

2021, Alberto scored 27 non-penalty goals in Serie A, and developed a reputation for his creativity by amassing 36 assists as Lazio's chief playmaker. He essentially developed into the player that Liverpool expected him to become in many ways, evolving into an inventive and progressive midfielder who thrived on the edge of the final third. Meanwhile, Aspas became his club's all-time top scorer by some distance. Across the six seasons between 2015 and 2021, he scored 79 non-penalty goals for Celta, who mostly finished below mid-table in La Liga.

The two players appeared on Comolli's radar because of the numbers behind their performances, and the same applied to Assaidi, who had accumulated 36 scoring returns in the Eredivisie as a youngster for Heerenveen in the two seasons prior to his Liverpool transfer. Comolli was picking up players who looked like hidden gems in the transfer market, but Assaidi ended up being sold to a club in the Middle East at the age of 26 after doing virtually nothing at Anfield. It was all about which young players on the continent looked good in the data. Years later, Alberto and Aspas justified Liverpool's early interest by showing up as effective players in Europe, but that development provided a lesson.

There are issues associated with signing players solely using numbers in football. Unlike baseball, which is a sport wedded to set-pieces, football incorporates far more intangible elements across the board. Alberto and Aspas couldn't speak English, for example, which was a problem considering the obvious importance of communication on and off the pitch, even if Rodgers did like to subtly remind people of his ability to speak Spanish every now and then.

They also seemed ill-suited to coping with the clichéd physical demands of the Premier League. English football has always been packed full of direct passes, aerial balls, crunching tackles and bad weather. Alberto and Aspas, for all their promise, lacked physicality. Steven Gerrard instantly judged his new team-mates after they joined, stating the pair 'looked about 15' when he first met them. 'Straightaway, as soon as I saw them in the dressing room, I knew they weren't going to make it in the Premier League,' he wrote in his autobiography. 'It boiled down to physique. They had the bodies of little boys.'

The brutish nature of the English game tends to be overplayed by the seasoned hardmen who survived and flourished, but it does seem to have an undeniable influence. 'In England, we all know what things players need to bring to the team: they need to be tall, they need to be quick, they need to be strong in the air,' said Peter Krawietz, who joined Liverpool in 2015 to work alongside Jürgen Klopp. Thiago Alcântara, who moved to Anfield as a midfielder in the summer of 2020, also noticed the change in demands upon his arrival. 'Throw-ins, corner kicks, goal kicks, everything happens at more speed here,' said the seven-time winner of the Bundesliga and four-time winner of La Liga. 'You have to adapt to that. When there is a situation where you think you can breathe, the ball is already in play again.' Felipe Anderson, who joined West Ham United from Lazio in 2018, claimed that when he first arrived in England, he couldn't initially last beyond the 70-minute mark. Fiyako Tomori moved from Chelsea to AC Milan in the January window of 2021, and he compared English football to basketball. 'Everything is end to end, there's more intensity,' he said. 'In Italy, it's more like American football. It's like you have plays. Everything is a bit more chilled. Everyone is walking a bit slower. Everything is just a bit calmer.'

In the summer of 2022, a player who looked like a Viking version of Andy Carroll arrived on English shores. He was 6ft 4in tall, muscular, powerful, and had impeccable blonde hair, which was long enough to fall beneath his shoulders. Manchester City needed a striker at the time, and they basically signed Thor to fill the void. He was Andy Carroll if Andy Carroll had been supercharged, painting himself as a giant who was faster than everyone else on the pitch. Even at the tender age of 21, Erling Haaland was accustomed to bullying his opponents, but even he felt the difference of playing football in England compared to Germany or Austria. 'Tougher, harder,' he said when asked about the Premier League after his debut campaign. 'I understand why people say it's the best league, because it really is. I love to play here. I like the duels, the running duels and everything. It's a really physical league, the tempo is amazing, something I like. A good duel is always nice. It's good to have a little bit of pain here and there.'

In 2020, Training Ground Guru used SkillCorner broadcast tracking data to conduct an analysis on the topic. Their study was spread across Europe's top five leagues and covered physical elements such as intensity, sprinting and overall volume. For intensity, which was determined by the average number of high-intensity activities and the average peak sprint velocity, the Premier League placed in a league of its own. For sprinting, which was determined by the average sprint distance and the average number of sprint activities, the Premier League again placed top. For overall volume, which was determined by the average total distance covered and the average high-intensity distance covered, the Premier League placed third for distance covered, but top for distance covered at a high intensity.

Comolli had bought players who appeared valuable upon first glance of the data and they would have been undervalued signings if their output had translated in England, but many of them simply weren't equipped to deliver enough of an immediate impression. There was logic behind investing in future stocks, but at a club the size of Liverpool – and in a competition as unforgiving as the Premier League – short-term performances still mattered, certainly to some extent. Considering the status of the Merseyside club near the top of the footballing food chain, Liverpool were in a strong enough position to let players develop elsewhere before later acquiring them to deliver their prime years of performance. Anfield had the potential to become a destination for players who were about to make the leap and experience their peak years.

Instead of purchasing players who needed five years before establishing any degree of consistency, the club needed to strike more of a Goldilocks balance in the transfer market. Not too young and not too old, but just right. 'Choosing players in any sport is an imperfect science,' said Henry. 'We certainly have been guilty of overspending on some players, and that can be tied to an analytical approach that hasn't worked well enough.' Indeed, in 2023, Klopp talked about Liverpool's precise approach in the market. 'The owners really want 200 games at 20 years old, that is pretty difficult,' he said. Experience is naturally valuable, because the greater the sample size attached to the profile of a player, the more accurate the read is likely to be regarding the details of their game. In order to gain that experience, though, players needed to age, hence the conflict.

The process is made even more complicated by the reality that every player matures at their own pace. In 2021, Vosse de Boode, head of sport science and data analytics at Ajax, talked about the concept of a biological age in a presentation at StatsBomb's annual football conference. She used two Dutch wonderkids to capture her point in Justin Kluivert and Matthijs de Ligt. The pair of Ajax prodigies were the same age at the time, but in a biological sense the former was a boy and the latter was a man. Kluivert is actually three months older than his Dutch team-mate, but he was still developing into an adult talent when he was a teenager. De Ligt, on the other hand, already stood around 6ft 2in tall and had the biological age of a player in his 20s. The art of identifying who's in the right spot to evolve and who hasn't yet reached that point is a tricky one to master but, regardless, Liverpool had to make improvements. They needed to begin covering every base when recruiting players. Signing unproven youngsters because of their reduced cost was not enough, and consulting data on its own was not enough.

Numerous English clubs have made comparable mistakes over the years. In 2015, Aston Villa attempted to navigate a transfer window by empowering data, with Patrick Riley, who had recently left his role of scouting coordinator at Liverpool, overseeing the change in approach as their new director of scouting and player recruitment. Riley worked alongside Sam Green at Villa Park, who joined from Opta and was appointed as head of research after being recommended by his Liverpool equivalent, Ian Graham. Speaking to *The Athletic* years later, Green shone a light on his methods at the time. 'Say we're looking for a midfielder,' he said. 'If he completes a pass sideways, that wouldn't impact his rating but winning a header from a set-piece or making an interception in the final third, would count for more. We would then combine everything the player does in the context of the game to get a goal value.'

Green was somewhat ahead of the curve at the time. Rather than using isolated event data to determine which players posted lots of shots or which players created lots of chances, he instead seemed intent on assessing performance as a whole in association with each player's overall impact on goals scored and goals conceded at the opposite end. The maths and physics graduate, who now heads up data science for Hawk-Eye, effectively attempted to recreate a model that Graham first constructed many years earlier while employed by Decision Technology.

Eight years after the 2002 World Cup, in which Henry Stott had underlined Senegal's 25 per cent chance of beating France, resulting in a partnership emerging with the Fink Tank, Castrol also seemed inspired by the data-fuelled insights firm. A sponsor for the 2010 World Cup, the oil company wanted to tap into numbers ahead of the big tournament, contracting Decision Technology to come up with a player rating system that would become known as the Castrol Index. Graham headed up the project, with players receiving points for each successful pass completed, depending on which zones of the pitch the ball was passed from and received in. Each zone was valued according to the percentage chance of scoring a goal from that part of the pitch. Misplaced and intercepted passes were penalised depending on how much danger those errors inflicted. Goalkeepers were punished for conceding shots that should have been saved, and defensive actions were rewarded depending on where they happened on the pitch. Conceding fouls and penalties also resulted in points deductions, with every player in the competition eventually awarded a score out of ten. It was an advanced means of evaluating performances, with players assessed based on all their actions rather than tackles, interceptions, passes, shots and the like being separated into discrete aspects of the game.

The Castrol Index was used for the Fink Tank beyond the World Cup, with player scores weighted for the difficulty of matches in different leagues. In November 2009, for example, Thierry Henry was ranked as the best player in Europe according to the system, followed by Cristiano Ronaldo and Lionel Messi, with the best player in the Premier League deemed to be Fernando Torres, who joined Chelsea a little over 12 months later. The Castrol Index wasn't too dissimilar to what Green later established at Villa, or what Graham later perfected on Merseyside. Beyond acting as a publicity stunt that featured Ronaldo wearing Castrol-sponsored clothing after winning his first Ballon d'Or, the ranking system didn't quite catch fire in the world of football. It wasn't created for recruitment, after all. If the product produced by the model was expressed in terms of each player's impact on goal difference or points in a league table, perhaps things might have been different but instead, players were judged out of ten to make the system easy to digest for the public. The method behind the process was scientific, but the end result had been trivialised.

Riley and Green were allegedly responsible for bringing several relatively unproven players to Villa Park, including Adama Traoré, Idrissa Gueye, Jordan Veretout, Jordan Ayew and Jordan Amavi. Each of those players experienced impressive careers after leaving Villa – similar to Aspas and Alberto with Liverpool – but at the time they were regarded as flops who struggled in England. Traoré later played for Wolves and Barcelona, albeit having only joined the latter on loan. Gueye joined Everton and then Paris Saint-Germain. Veretout spent his prime in Serie A at Fiorentina and AS Roma. The players weren't bad, their moves just didn't work out for one reason or another. Tim Sherwood played the role of an extreme version of Brendan Rodgers at Villa. The loyal patriot believed every cliché under the sun about his beloved Premier League. He wanted players who could fight, scrap and benefit from 'knowing' the competition, whatever that means. To appease him, the club tended to his needs by purchasing Joleon Lescott, Micah Richards and Rudi Gestede. By the end of October, Sherwood had been sacked, and less than a year later Riley followed him out the door.

Good players aren't guaranteed to succeed. Villa invested funds in several talents who proceeded to eventually prove their worth, but as part of a squad in 2015/16 they accumulated just 17 points, losing 27 of their

38 matches. Only three teams in Premier League history have amassed fewer points than Villa did that season. Liverpool had mounting evidence to suggest that data was capable of providing valuable insight, but it couldn't be used in isolation when recruiting players. No stone could be left unturned. There were no shortcuts. It was simply too easy for a football transfer to fail.

Chapter Seven
Jürgen

FIVE YEARS of ownership under FSG had passed, yet Liverpool had very little to show for it. Aside from one League Cup delivered by Kenny Dalglish, the Reds hadn't won an ounce of silverware, and they didn't appear particularly close either. Brendan Rodgers had left Liverpool without an identity and, as a consequence of his blurred direction by the end of his tenure, the squad he left behind was a mishmash of different styles and formations. Success in football was proving to be considerably more difficult to achieve than in baseball, and data in the sport was still packed full of stigmas. The narrative suggested that Liverpool had stood still by wandering around in the dark for years under FSG, but in reality the people in charge had benefited from a whole string of valuable lessons. You have to learn how to walk before you run. The dos and don'ts were more apparent than ever and Liverpool had a clean slate from which to essentially reset and start again, but this time with the necessary infrastructure already behind them. In their search for a successor to Rodgers, Liverpool didn't need a mathematical genius at the helm to begin making scientific football decisions, just somebody who would listen, while ideally getting the most from the players at his disposal.

Their managerial shortlist consisted of three names: Eddie Howe, Carlo Ancelotti and Jürgen Klopp. Ancelotti had the most decorated record of the trio in terms of winning honours at the pinnacle of the sport, but Liverpool weren't ready to win. The cultured Italian was known for thriving when able to act as the icing on the cake by adding finishing touches, but Liverpool still needed to bake their cake. Ancelotti was a Michelin-starred chef who was accustomed to cooking with the finest ingredients, but he wouldn't be presented with that luxury at Anfield, at least not for a few years. Klopp, on the other hand, was emerging with a reputation for harvesting the absolute maximum from whatever he was afforded, and he was available, having resigned from his post at Borussia Dortmund just four months earlier. A covert summit was scheduled in New York between FSG and the German coach, and days later he was appointed to lead Liverpool's much-delayed comeback. The rebirth would be designed based on previous lessons. It was time for FSG to deliver their vision. Liverpool hadn't lost faith in the worth of numbers, but they had gathered information about how to better use them in a footballing context, while perfecting their hierarchy and structure behind the scenes. And as a result of technological advancements in the space, the data available to people in the sport was far more complex and sophisticated in comparison to when FSG first descended on Merseyside in 2010.

Klopp was a one-off. He almost seemed purpose-built, like he had been constructed in a laboratory to be the best possible candidate for every aspect of the job at Anfield. He genuinely could have been a comic book character. Klopp stood around 6ft 3in tall, sported a tracksuit and baseball cap on the sidelines – which conflicted with the English tradition of wearing a shirt and tie – and his bold glasses were as unmistakable as his infectious laugh. His distinct appearance was just the tip of the iceberg. Klopp was renowned for his magnetism. If he was in the room, everybody knew about it. İlkay Gündoğan, who played under Klopp for four years, described him as a 'father figure' who treated his players almost like his friends. 'I'm their friend, but not their best friend,' he once said as Liverpool prepared to face Barcelona in a Champions League semi-final in 2019. Unlike those who came before him, Klopp had all of the necessary dynamism to adequately personify the proud and fiery nature of the socialist city that his club represented. He had a fighting spirit. He was fearless, charismatic and daring, and his brand of football upheld similar values.

Klopp arrived in England as somewhat of a tactical pioneer. Football in the Premier League conventionally followed a familiar pattern on the pitch, which consisted of having the ball, losing the ball and retreating into a sturdy defensive block until the ball was regained, before restarting that process. The large majority of teams generally behaved in accordance with the design, with Gérard Houllier and Rafael Benítez very much reinforcing the theme during their spells in charge of Liverpool, but Klopp wanted to disrupt it. Whenever his players lost the ball, he advised against transitioning into a passive defensive block. Instead, he wanted his players to be proactive by chasing the ball to regain it as quickly as possible. His players hunted in packs and focused on zonally occupying the space around the opponent who had the ball, rather than man-marking his nearby team-mates.

'The best moment to win the ball is immediately after your team just lost it,' Klopp said. 'The opponent is still looking for orientation. He will have taken his eyes off the game to make his tackle or interception, and he will have expended energy. Both make him vulnerable.' Once regaining possession, Klopp instructed his players to essentially seize the moment and go for the throat. He didn't want possession to be recirculated. He didn't want another long sequence to be constructed. He wanted blood, and he wanted it as quickly as possible. Klopp's name became associated with chaos because of the crux of his idea. His players were instructed to win the ball straight after losing it and, once doing so, he believed that moment of disorganisation was the perfect time to penetrate and score. The product on the pitch could almost resemble basketball at times, as it was packed full of turnovers, direct passes and loose balls. Klopp didn't have much of an initial interest in governing possession, it wasn't his thing. 'I don't like winning with 80 per cent of the ball,' he said. 'Fighting football, not serenity football, everybody is dirty in the face and goes home and cannot play for the next four weeks, that is what I like.'

His cut-throat approach allowed him to conquer the Bundesliga with Dortmund in two consecutive seasons, ahead of the mighty Bayern Munich. Klopp's pressing game was destined to prosper against titans such as Bayern, who were accustomed to controlling proceedings and seeing most of the ball. Between 2010 and 2012, his Dortmund outfit won five matches in a row against Bayern in all competitions, despite their status as relative underdogs. Bayern reached a point where they effectively started to play football with fear against their arch-rivals. Dortmund had grown famous for being clinical, fast, intense and efficient. One insignificant mistake on the ball would be enough for Klopp's men to spring forward and pounce. 'Umschaltspiel' was his response in his very first press conference on Merseyside when asked to describe his playing style, which is a German word that loosely translates into 'switching game' in English, or, in footballing terms, 'transition play'. Whenever the match was in an uncertain state of flux on the pitch, that's when Dortmund would flourish.

Klopp's football was modern and radical, and it was executed by players who truly wanted to play for him. He was a natural communicator who cherished the human elements of the sport. 'You cannot win without tactical things, but the emotion makes the difference,' he once said in an interview with the BBC. 'The first time I met him, it was the aura, the presence,' said Jordan Henderson when asked to reflect on Klopp towards the end of his time as captain of Liverpool. 'Everything about him, it just felt special.' Klopp's vital team talk in the nervy minutes leading up to the final of the Champions League in 2018 perhaps captures the eccentric and playful nature of his character. Liverpool were about to face the frightening task of competing against Real Madrid in Kyiv, who had won the prestigious tournament in each of the previous two campaigns. It was a daunting prospect, with Klopp sensing the need to downplay the occasion as a means of relaxing his players. The room fell silent, but before he opened his mouth he proceeded to tuck his New Balance top into his underwear, revealing his CR7-branded boxer shorts. The changing room erupted with laughter. Ronaldo failed to score in that final, although Madrid did manage to win by three goals to one. Klopp was easy to like. His players were willing to run through brick walls for him, as the old cliché goes, and as a former student of sports science he was keen to present them with the necessary support to perform to such an intense physical level.

Oliver Bartlett worked as a fitness coach at Dortmund during Klopp's tenure. Speaking in an interview with StatsBomb, he recalled his specific demands and how they related to his playing style on the pitch. 'At the time, Klopp wanted every player to get physically involved,' said Bartlett. 'Move up the field, move down the field. All positions at a very high physical level. That was something we worked towards with the whole team. We had centre-backs doing quite a bit of running and acceleration drills, which not every team was doing. It was specific for the style.' Bartlett even attempted to improve the pace and acceleration of Nuri Şahin, who spent six months on loan at Liverpool under Rodgers in 2012/13, because Klopp regarded him as too immobile for his intentions.

The charismatic German seemed to be the full package, and he even jumped at the chance to work alongside a sporting director. Unlike Rodgers, who essentially considered himself as a mastermind in many ways, Klopp knew his limitations and didn't shy away from asking for help. 'It's no secret I like the concept of a sporting director,' he said upon his appointment at Anfield. 'Having worked under this model previously, I have found it to be nothing but positive. I don't want to deal with players' agents on a daily basis. I really think that takes energy away from the really important stuff that you have to do.' The 'first and last word' regarding transfers was all Klopp required. 'I'm not an idiot,' he said in his first press conference. 'For me, it's enough, and in the middle we can discuss everything. We only want to discuss very good players. I'm not a genius. I don't know more than the rest of the world. I need the other people to get the perfect information and when we have this we will sign a player or sell a player.'

The difference between the new man and his predecessor was clear before any football had even been played. Liverpool had acquired a true leader. An elite coach who was willing to empower those around him. In essence, a transfer committee of sorts would remain in place behind the scenes despite the popular failure of the concept under Rodgers, but it would no longer consist of a battle of wits or operate under the same name. Klopp would listen to those around him. Their opinions mattered. 'My confidence is big enough that I can really let people grow next to me. I need experts around me. Have strong people around you with better knowledge in different departments, don't act like you know everything, and be ready to admit that,' he once said when asked about the concept of leadership.

From the beginning, Klopp began shaping his blueprint at Liverpool. His first match in charge was away against Tottenham Hotspur, who were developing into one of the Premier League's best teams under Mauricio

Pochettino. For 90 minutes, his players ran like they were possessed, covering more distance than in any of their previous matches under Rodgers that season and also becoming the first team to outrun Spurs. Klopp's presence had swiftly injected a degree of intensity to Liverpool's game, but the unforgiving tempo had a detrimental impact on their use of the ball. 'There were many full-throttle moments in the game. We were a little bit nervous when we got the ball because the pulse was a little too high at this moment,' he said.

Supporters had witnessed a half-baked version of what was to come. The Reds would attempt to become an upgraded version of Dortmund by employing a comparable tactical approach without having to sell their stars at the end of every season. At one point early in Klopp's tenure, the word 'terrible' was written in block capitals on a whiteboard at the club's training ground. It was described as how opponents would feel after going toe to toe with Liverpool for 90 minutes. Andreas Kornmayer and Mona Nemmer were quickly installed as Klopp's fitness experts shortly after his appointment. The duo were poached from Bayern, with Kornmayer appointed as head of fitness and conditioning, while Nemmer started work as head of nutrition. Klopp had begun assembling his team of experts. The team behind the team.

Roberto Firmino, who was signed alongside Christian Benteke under Rodgers in his final window at the club, hadn't started well at his new club. As a so-called 'committee signing', Rodgers didn't seem to appreciate his skill set and he used him in numerous different ways in search of his best role, including as a wide player on both flanks and as a number ten. There wasn't much of a plan for his evolution at his new club, but Klopp was familiar with him after the pair had competed as opponents in the Bundesliga. He had even once explored the possibility of signing him, but Dortmund simply couldn't afford him. Henderson later confessed to not knowing much about Firmino after he moved to England. 'You could see that he had quality. It was tough for him at the beginning but I can always remember when Jürgen did come in, he was the one player that he seemed really excited about.'

It didn't take long for Firmino to be awarded the No.9 shirt at Anfield. Benteke, who stood around 6ft 3in tall, was simply too rigid for Klopp's fluid and lively style, and Daniel Sturridge wasn't robust or intense enough to cope with his physical demands on a consistent basis. Firmino wasn't much of a scorer and lacked the speed to threaten open spaces behind defenders, but the Brazilian was as industrious as they come and his technical level was outstanding. 'Bobby was in all of the ideas I had about how we could play,' said Klopp when Firmino called time on his Liverpool career in 2023. 'If you would have seen me alone in the office with the tactics board, it was constantly "Bobby here, Bobby there", just because of his natural skill set.'

One way or another, the system would be constructed around him, considering he was just 23 years old. He was nothing like the stereotypical striker who had graced the English game over the years, but he was worth accommodating in Klopp's eyes. From Gary Lineker to Ian Wright to Robbie Fowler to Alan Shearer to Michael Owen, strikers were supposed to score goals. They came alive in the penalty area. English football was a breeding ground for the age-old fox in the box. Strikers finished moves and did very little else, but Klopp's main man was different. 'He sacrifices himself for the team, he doesn't really care about scoring that much,' said Mohamed Salah, who arguably became the main beneficiary of Firmino's generous nature on the pitch.

His No.9 shirt was a smokescreen. The number on his jersey suggested that he would behave in a certain manner and fulfil a particular role, but it was little more than a disguise. Firmino did exactly what he was good at, which involved linking with others in tight spaces, retreating into midfield and generating space for others. He contributed across the board rather than dedicating all his energy towards accumulating shots, eventually becoming associated with pressing because of his role as Liverpool's leader of the pack. As the team's most advanced player in terms of positioning on paper, Firmino would become Liverpool's first line of defence. Klopp would later label the South American as his 'connector', while also describing him as a 'ball chaser' and the best 'offensive defender' he's ever seen. 'A football team is like an orchestra, you have different people for different instruments,' said Klopp. 'Bobby plays like 12 instruments in our orchestra.' He was the first piece of Klopp's puzzle, with the rest of his teammates arriving over time via the transfer market and the club's academy.

Klopp's crystal-clear identity as a coach would aid Liverpool's scouting process. Every player who played for him had to be intense, physical and – perhaps more obviously – very good. He considered himself as a trainer rather than a big spender. 'I'm completely different to the English philosophy of we have to buy, we have to buy, all about transfers, all about transfers, because I believe in training,' he said. Liverpool began to prioritise only the finest gems in the transfer market using key performance indicators associated with Klopp's game. Quality was more important than quantity, and scouting was made far easier because of the clarity of his tactical vision.

FSG had found their kingpin. The man who would proceed to link every department together as the face of the operation. They had struck gold. Klopp was a listener, and he was a leader. A contemporary tactician who was emotionally intelligent with a proven record of improving teams and players once presented with time. He wasn't much of a data guy but that didn't matter, he was open-minded enough to pay attention. He was surprised to learn that underlying statistics had actually played a part in his own appointment. Liverpool had crunched the numbers posted by Klopp's Dortmund team to determine the level at which they had performed. The club's head of research conducted the study. His name was Ian Graham.

Chapter Eight

Einstein

MICHAEL EDWARDS boarded an eight-hour flight shortly after joining Liverpool in 2011. He was heading to the US to attend the MIT Sloan Sports Analytics Conference in Boston, Massachusetts. Regarded as the must-attend event on the calendar for those in the field, and known as 'Sloan' in short, it was founded in 2006 by Daryl Morey as a means of providing a forum for industry professionals, aspiring students and fans of the sport. As Liverpool's head of analysis, it was the responsibility of Edwards to keep his finger on the pulse. He had to be in the know about new developments in his area of expertise. He wanted to be ahead of the curve and would continue to attend sports conferences as Liverpool's sporting director – usually under a fake name – over ten years later, always as a spectator rather than a speaker in fitting with his under-the-radar profile.

Edwards wasn't alone for his long-haul journey to the US. He was accompanied by Ian Graham, with whom he had developed a professional relationship during Damien Comolli's spell as sporting director at Tottenham

Hotspur. After the Frenchman departed from his role, the relationship between Spurs and Graham's employers, Decision Technology, continued for a short period, with Edwards acting as the main point of contact at White Hart Lane. A doctor in the field of polymer physics, Graham had effectively stumbled upon the world of sport after completing his PhD at the University of Cambridge in 2005. Unmotivated by a career in academia, he was forwarded a job advert by his girlfriend, which touted a position involving football statistics. The role was posted by Decision Technology and Graham was awarded the position after applying. By 2006, he was put in direct contact with Edwards and tasked with completing numerous one-off projects.

Daniel Levy was cautiously guiding Spurs towards more of a data-driven approach, appointing Comolli and Edwards while also establishing an exclusive deal with Decision Technology, who were consequently unable to work with any rival institution in the Premier League due to the terms of their contract. 'It was a consultancy deal where we'd do player analysis, giving recruitment advice and that sort of thing,' Graham later said. 'It was kind of like whatever they needed from us, they could ask and we'd try to apply our data analysis to it.'

Graham was glad to be involved with Spurs. It was a step up from his weekly contributions to the Fink Tank – which he did for six and a half years – and it was more engaging to him than a life in the classroom. A Welshman who had a natural affinity with numbers, Graham was a football fan growing up but also had a vague interest in American sports, particularly those that embraced statistics. Alongside his contributions to Spurs, Decision Technology and the Fink Tank, he also created a lesser-known blog in 2006. 'Fed up with pundits talking nonsense? You've come to the right place', he wrote as his website's tagline. For a period of around 18 months, Graham journaled his musings about the sport. He applied data to popular and relevant topics of conversation, with his first post dedicated to West Ham United. His thorough but concise deconstruction of the Hammers was relatively trailblazing back then. He was among the first in a public space to evaluate a team in the Premier League using data to accurately understand their fortunes. Twitter and Facebook had only just been created, so there wasn't much of a platform for Graham to share ideas with like-minded people, and data in football was still in its infancy. Nevertheless, the crux of his analysis was that West Ham didn't create enough shots, and they allowed too many on the defensive side of the game. 'Last season, that didn't matter because they converted chances into goals very well, and their keepers kept out all of those shots,' he wrote, but that was no longer happening, hence their sudden decline towards the relegation zone.

West Ham hadn't technically got any worse in a performance capacity, but their players at both ends of the pitch had simply lost the ability to perform beyond expectation. After finishing ninth in the Premier League in the previous year, they had seemingly fallen off a cliff by dropping towards the foot of the table. In reality, though, not that much had changed under the hood. Graham was able to use numbers to cut through the noise, even concluding his piece by naming the positive and negative contributors within Alan Pardew's squad. Daniel Gabbidon was worth 8.45 points per season according to Graham's findings, whereas Paul Konchesky, who Liverpool later proceeded to sign in their final window under Tom Hicks and George Gillett, managed to cost the Hammers 7.64 points per season. He also blogged about whether Rangers were right to sack Paul Le Guen. 'My guess is that short-term – less than ten games – blips in form result in upset fans, and calls for the manager's head. The directors duly comply. Rash decisions and short-termism seems to be behind a lot of manager sackings,' he wrote in his conclusion.

When John Henry proceeded to acquire Liverpool as part of FSG in 2010, Graham took note from afar. 'Liverpool is the place to be,' he later confessed to have thought at the time, knowing all about the story of *Moneyball* and Henry's historic underlying belief in using data to gain an edge. Graham anticipated Anfield becoming the capital of such practices in the footballing world, and he wasn't wrong. Once Edwards moved away from Spurs, having followed Comolli to Liverpool, he remained in touch with Graham due to his belief that he was the best in the business. Liverpool were restricted from working directly with Decision Technology because of the company's ongoing agreement with Spurs but, nevertheless, the duo kept in contact.

Henry first attempted to navigate the roadblock by absorbing the company and doing what Levy never did by purchasing Decision Technology outright, but founder Henry Stott had reservations due to his established agreement with Spurs. Henry respected his decision and instead decided to change his tactics by specifically headhunting Graham through Edwards. Liverpool deliberately bypassed Decision Technology, and throughout the course of their business trip to Boston, Edwards attempted to convince his former colleague to quit his job so that he could link up with him at Anfield. It didn't take much effort. By pure coincidence, Graham happened to be a lifelong Liverpool supporter. He had been working on modelling for ten years, he was one of the first of his kind as a scientist working in football, and after conversing with Edwards at 37,000 feet above the ground, he agreed to become Liverpool's first-ever director of research, with Spurs and Decision Technology later informed upon his return to England.

FSG had appointed Comolli, Comolli had appointed Edwards, and Edwards had effectively appointed Graham. Liverpool were getting somewhere. The backroom team behind the backroom team was taking shape, but there was a long way to go, it would be a lengthy process. 'We'll look at stats no one else will look at, employ scouting in a way that has a compelling organisational context, question everything and everyone and ensure we have the best player development curriculum and protocols,' said Henry. 'In short, we are determined to outwork everyone else and hopefully be smarter every year.' It sounded great, but was it realistic? To establish such an advantage, Liverpool had to start from scratch. A clean slate was required. There was no analysis department at this point, and there was no data science department, either. Later described by Edwards in his departure letter as Liverpool's 'stats man', Graham informed the owners that building everything up from the ground would take about a year, stating that nobody should expect to hear from him for at least six months. 'Fine,' they responded.

It was a long-term decision that hadn't previously been made in England. Aside from Arsenal's purchase of StatDNA in late 2012 for over £2m, no club had truly explored the prospect of possessing their own custom-made department dedicated to data science and analytics. Using external providers such as Prozone and Opta to gather detailed information was far more common. Liverpool were willing to be patient with tomorrow in mind, and the possibilities were endless, but the primary focus at the beginning was transfers. Recruitment, according to Graham, was the reason he was brought in. For the 12 months following his appointment, he dedicated virtually all of his time to building scouting applications. His belief that his department should primarily focus on the transfer market hasn't wilted throughout his stay on Merseyside. 'Any analyst not working on recruitment is literally wasting their time,' he said on stage at Stamford Bridge during StatsBomb's football conference in 2021. 'In terms of impact versus costs, recruitment and squad planning is where you can make the maximum impact,' he said, when speaking at the *Financial Times*' Business of Football Summit in 2022.

Insights from data can be harnessed across numerous different departments within the confines of a football club, but he's always judged recruitment to be the most worthwhile in terms of notable returns in a financial sense. 'In sport, there is this concept of marginal gains,' said Graham. 'The idea is if you can find a one per cent edge, that makes you one per cent better. If you can find ten, that makes you ten per cent better. In some sports that might work well but football is nowhere near being an optimised sport. You don't have to worry about marginal gains, you should look at all of the possible gains, pick the biggest one and ignore everything else.' That was exactly what Liverpool attempted to do from the start, but the transfer budget and the quality of readily available data proved to be a problem, as did Brendan Rodgers and Andy Carroll for different reasons.

Liverpool showcased a clear interest in chances created during Comolli's early spell in charge of recruitment, but Graham needed to go much deeper. It wasn't enough. 'Every business has metrics that correlate to success,' Billy Beane once said. 'It's just finding them, which ones are the most valuable, which ones do you invest in and which ones you get a return on.' Graham had to identify the equivalent of OBP or Wins Above Replacement, a metric that arrived in baseball further down the line and involved measuring a player's value in all facets of the game by determining how many more wins he was worth than a replacement-level player in the same position – if such a thing even existed in football. The sport was becoming packed full of metrics, from tackles to clearances to passes into the final third to crosses into the penalty box to shots to expected goals, and some were more valuable than others. Graham needed to find a way of grouping everything together as part of one divine stat, almost like he did for the Castrol Index, so he began to fixate his attention on goal difference and each individual player's impact on picking up points, building on the work that was initially teased in his amateur blog.

Football is a complicated game. It's unpredictable. It's volatile. It doesn't make sense. Morey once captured the headline problem with using basic numbers to analyse a low-scoring sport such as football in comparison to his beloved basketball. 'It's very complex. Lots of free moving, not a lot of set things,' he said at Sloan in 2019. 'Every time something happens, you get zero. How are you concluding anything if everything leads to zero? You could do everything right and get zero. You could do everything wrong and get zero.' Despite the noise surrounding everything that happens on the pitch, only one thing really matters: goals. The fundamental team objective is to score goals at one end of the pitch, while conceding as little as possible at the opposite end. Score more, concede less, eureka.

Improving team performance, primarily through recruitment, formed the crux of Graham's remit, and if team performance was essentially defined by scoring more while conceding less, improving goal difference was his underlying aim. 'People don't like the theory that the best players win the game,' he said in an interview with ESPN in 2023. 'People love to mystify that there has to be some magic about football that's not easy to measure.' He labelled goal difference as a 'language' used behind the scenes at Liverpool. Decisions were made with a view to improving the goal difference of the team, which should in turn have an impact on points, wins and – if all goes according to plan – trophies. 'We spend a lot of time trying to have one football language to speak in, so we speak in terms of goal difference as getting a high goal difference is what wins you more games,' Graham said. 'Our ratings for players are in terms of how much goal difference they will add to a team and that can be split up into many different factors to tell us how they are providing that goal difference. In order to get a list of players from 1 to 100, it is the first thing you rank them on. If they come to Liverpool, how will they improve the team and the goal difference?'

The level of certain players is fairly obvious. Even the uninitiated man on the street would be just fine determining that Lionel Messi is good at football upon watching him play. A professional scout would undoubtedly provide more granular detail upon inspection of Messi's game, but data is required to place a numerical value on his influence. How much of an impact would Messi have on Liverpool's goal difference or points tally if he was to start wearing red? Your typical scout would have an answer, but it would be an educated guess based on pure intuition and experience. Graham's modelling allowed Liverpool to determine such insights using predictive mathematics. His findings contributed to the decisions made by Edwards regarding the squad and the biggest areas of improvement to address in each passing transfer window.

Messi was once used as an example by Graham as he outlined the purpose of his job. 'With "Moneyball", which isn't a word that we use very often, the point is not improvement in performance,' said Graham. 'Anybody can improve performance by signing Messi, for example. "Moneyball" is about maximising your improvement in performance for a minimum cost, and that is not to say we are cheap.' Under FSG, Liverpool were intent on improving performance as efficiently as possible and Graham's work allowed the club to forecast outcomes before making informed moves in the transfer market. Liverpool didn't tend to spend as much as some of their heavyweight rivals in England, but their search for the biggest achievable gains was constant.

Graham told his audience at Stamford Bridge in 2021:

> We can see the distribution of goal difference impact of players for each Premier League team. The better players add goal difference for Liverpool and Manchester City near the top compared to the average player, and you've got teams at the bottom who generally have players who cost you a little bit of goal difference per game. The interesting thing is there are some players at mid-table teams who would be above average at Champions League teams, and you've got some players at Champions League teams who would only be average at mid-table teams. You can compare each player to his own teammates. The typical spread in performance is about 0.08 goal difference per game. What does that mean? A 30th-percentile player costs you 0.04, a 70th-percentile player gains you 0.04. Replacing a 30th with a 70th gains you 0.08 and that is the typical spread that you see in a Premier League team. +0.08 goal difference per game equates to two points per season. And that is replacing a 30th with a 70th, so they aren't extremely good or extremely bad players. If you can replace a 15th-percentile player with a 85th-percentile player, that's more like an extra four

or five points per season. You're making many of these recruitment decisions per season.

As Graham's infrastructure and applications strengthened in the years after his appointment, his analysis played a part in the recruitment of Jürgen Klopp in 2015. The German had transformed the status of Borussia Dortmund from mid-table mediocrity to Champions League finalists over a five-year period, but his final campaign in charge was troublesome. At the midpoint of the season, Klopp's team were in the relegation zone of the Bundesliga table. They had amassed just 15 points from a possible 51, which was the joint-fewest alongside Freiburg. Liverpool needed to know more. Klopp was on the shortlist of possible replacements for Rodgers, but his most recent campaign in management seemed to be a failure, and it forced him to announce his resignation three years before his contract was due to end. Graham's analysis allowed Liverpool to learn that Dortmund suffered from bad fortune rather than bad coaching. 'His last season in Dortmund was disastrous, but our analysis showed something completely different,' Graham told Stephen Dubner on the *Freakonomics Radio* podcast. 'They were still clearly the second-best team in Germany, but the performances did not match the results. I analysed ten seasons of Bundesliga performances and Dortmund were the second-unluckiest team in that ten-year history.'

Graham didn't just conduct his own analysis. He read the work of others, including an article produced by Colin Trainor, who analysed the topic in 2014. A finance director with a passion for deconstructing sports in his spare time,

Trainor once acted as a consultant for an unnamed Premier League club. In fact, he recommended his employers to sign a certain Naby Këita, who was contracted to Red Bull Salzburg at the time, in the January transfer window of 2016, but nothing materialised and the Guinean moved to Liverpool two and a half years later. Like Graham, Trainor found Klopp's team to be unfortunate in their opening 17 fixtures before the winter break, particularly in both penalty boxes. 'The use of analytics can help us begin to make assessments about whether certain results have arisen from great skill or were possibly due to some combination of fortuitous circumstances,' he wrote.

Trainor used expected goals to determine whether the quality of shooting in Dortmund's matches had distorted the landscape, and it had. In attack, Klopp's team had generated shots worth roughly 25 goals, according to his model, whereas in defence they had allowed their opponents to produce efforts worth around 17 goals. In reality, though, Dortmund had scored just 18 times while conceding 26. His model suggested that if shot conversion had been normal at both ends of the pitch, Klopp's team would have amassed around double the number of points, ranking fourth in the table rather than 17th. Dortmund struggled to convert their shots into goals, their opponents did not, primarily because of Roman Weidenfeller's poor goalkeeping, and losses naturally followed. Even the best coach in the world can't score goals, he's reliant on his players to finish their chances. The best coach in the world can't save shots either; he's reliant on his goalkeeper to at least perform to an average standard between the sticks.

Some clubs might have been inclined to overlook Klopp due to the turbulence attached to his final campaign in the German top flight, but Liverpool were confident that he was the ideal candidate, and Graham's findings only reinforced that belief. Like Rodgers at Swansea, his managerial impact at Dortmund was indisputable, and he also had quite an influence on Mainz in his first job in management. 'Obviously, it's a great thing to win the Champions League, but my greatest success as a coach was promotion to the Bundesliga with Mainz in 2004,' said Klopp in 2019. The evidence behind his success in Germany suggested that his impact on team performance was almost unrivalled across Europe. Once he was acquired in 2015, Graham's advice – fuelled by goal difference – would form an integral part of the club's scouting methods. He would feed Edwards with the information that he required to make sensible and evidence-based choices. Decisions surrounding Klopp's squad and how it would be constructed incorporated analytics alongside traditional methods. It took plenty of time and years of ironing out the kinks, but Liverpool suddenly had everything in place to merge the analogue with the digital, and they had a coach who was willing to listen.

Chapter Nine

Truth Serum

IN 2019, RunRepeat conducted a study surrounding the presence of bias in football. The Danish research firm analysed 2,073 statements from commentators in 80 football matches, discussing 643 unique players of various races and skin tones. Their findings suggested that, when talking about intelligence, 62.6 per cent of praise was directed at players with lighter skin, whereas 63.3 per cent of criticism was aimed at those with darker skin. When speaking about power, commentators were around 6.6 times more likely to be talking about players with darker skin tones. When talking about work ethic, 60.4 per cent of praise was aimed at players with lighter skin tones.

Bias is far and wide in sport, and it comes in numerous different forms. Arsenal once passed up on the opportunity to sign Virgil van Dijk because he was deemed to be 'too nonchalant' by Steve Rowley, their leading scout, upon inspection of his game during his time at Celtic. Who could forget Matthijs de Ligt's claims that a club once opted against signing him from Ajax because his father was regarded as 'too fat' and the club in question feared that he was destined to follow in his footsteps?

Whether it's conscious or unconscious, players are often judged and evaluated because of irrelevancies. Too much attention tends to be given to details that simply don't matter. If a football player decides to wear gloves on the pitch, they can be sure that some spectators, including scouts, will derive conclusions about elements of their character. A male player's hairstyle can impact how he's perceived, and the same goes for whether a player is inclined to shout at their team-mates or not. From a player's nationality to the colour of their football boots to the number of cars in the garage to whether or not they watch football in their spare time, opinions are forever being shaped. The infamous and perhaps exaggerated recruitment scene in *Moneyball* involves scouts coming to conclusions about a baseball player because of the shape of his jawline and the appearance of his girlfriend. Some elements matter, others certainly do not.

Between October 2015 and February 2022, Liverpool bought 23 players for Jürgen Klopp, including free transfers. Ian Graham's favourite signings were those that likely wouldn't have otherwise happened without his expert assistance. He has a thing for players who tend to drift under the radar, and he's publicly confessed as much. Data allows him to cut through the bias attached to scouting for talent. 'I don't like video, it biases you,' he told the *New York Times*. His thoughts on players are almost exclusively determined by statistics. After watching Naby Keïta perform against Leicester City in 2018, Graham was asked whether the Guinean midfielder had played well against the Foxes by his interviewer, Bruce Schoenfeld. He wouldn't respond with an answer until he had consulted the data the following day.

'The players I really like are those who shine through in the data, but don't naturally shine through for your typical football fan or scout,' he said. 'Awkward, ungainly players, or players who have been overlooked, for various other purposes.' Keïta was one of Graham's leading lights. He was an analytics darling who portrayed himself as a restless, all-action midfielder in the numbers. The norm for most players was to add to their team's goal difference by contributing in attack or defence, but Keïta dazzled across the board. The numbers depicted him as an outlier in comparison to his peers. 'We try to put everything into one currency, so football is measured in goals, it's what gets you a win,' said Graham. 'We try to take whatever action a player does on a pitch – a pass, a shot, a tackle if you're a defender – and ask the question: what was this team's chance of scoring a goal before this action happened, and what was the team's chance of scoring a goal after that action happened? We call that Goal Probability Added.'

Keïta was always best loved by those who consulted data before forming their opinions. StatsBomb's Ted Knutson produced an article in 2016 on possible midfield reinforcements for Arsenal. 'If I am buying one central midfielder in Europe right now, it's Naby Keïta,' he wrote. 'Need a DM? Naby Keïta. Need an 8? Naby Keïta. A 10 that scores, creates and destroys? Na-bee Kay-tuh'. The far-reaching scouting network of Red Bull had possession of his services at the time. He spent two years in Salzburg between 2014 and 2016, before switching to Leipzig to test his qualities against better players in Germany, all while executing an intense playing style to uphold the values of Red Bull as an energy drink brand. He was athletic, dynamic and unpredictable, and whether Keïta was fielded in deeper areas or further forward, his influence was always noticeable, particularly in the numbers.

Truth be told, his uniqueness in comparison to his peers was obvious enough to grab the attention of most spectators, but it was the data that convinced Liverpool to go the extra mile. RB Leipzig initially refused to sanction his departure. Ralf Rangnick was in charge of the whole Red Bull operation at the time, and he felt one more year in Germany – coupled with exposure in the Champions League – would only add value to his profile, but Liverpool were willing to push the boat out. As the deadline of the summer transfer window of 2017 approached, Michael Edwards agreed a club-record deal for Keïta. He wouldn't arrive on Merseyside for another year because of Leipzig's demands, but that didn't bother Liverpool's recruitment team. He was deemed to be worth the wait, although it remains to be seen whether Edwards would have agreed to such unusual terms if Keïta hadn't appeared as such a rare breed in Graham's database.

Once he arrived, the Guinean midfielder proceeded to become quite a topic of conversation among supporters over the course of his five years in a red shirt, almost emerging into yet another piece of ammunition for the traditionalists to use in their rage against the use of numbers in football. Keïta was understood to be a data-driven capture and arrived as the most expensive midfielder in Liverpool's history. He also took Steven Gerrard's famous No.8 shirt, so supporters naturally expected to see his reincarnation. Spectators inside Anfield awaited goals, assists, power, marauding runs and dynamic moments of individual brilliance in the clutch, but a swarm of injuries throughout his five-year stay prevented him from being presented with the keys to the team.

In Liverpool's very first Premier League match with Keïta in the building, Klopp selected him ahead of captain Jordan Henderson, who started on the bench. The African midfielder repaid his faith, shining in a dominant 4-0 win over West Ham United and painting himself as the future of his team's engine room. He was everywhere. 'I'm surprised how good he is, if I'm honest,' said striker Daniel Sturridge when asked about his new team-mate. 'I knew he was good but I don't watch German football too often. I haven't seen a midfielder like him for a while, he is something different. It's crazy. The things he can do with the ball, he can defend, he can pass, he can dribble, he is fast, he is strong. He has got everything.' The following week, Keïta started ahead of Henderson once again in a clash against Crystal Palace, and the same happened five days later against Brighton & Hove Albion. Klopp had a midfield department that exuded industry and effort, but now he was benefiting from the option of a talent who was equally as intense, but a lot more enterprising with the ball at his feet.

All was going according to plan before Keïta picked up his first setback at Liverpool just eight matches into his first Premier League campaign. His next came in March, followed by another in May. Keïta was injured for the start of the following season, and with Trent Alexander-Arnold and Andy Robertson quietly establishing themselves as full-back creators who rarely missed a single minute of action, Klopp's blueprint for the development of his team was cautiously changing. With Liverpool's playmaking full-back duo growing in prominence, the need for an expressive and audacious midfielder like Keïta was lessening. Klopp suddenly required little more than a safety net in the middle of the park, with Henderson thriving as a functional presence who simply did a job for the team alongside Gini Wijnaldum and Fabinho. Keïta was almost tasked with playing within himself whenever he was free from injuries and presented with game time. His ball-winning tendencies still proved to be valuable, but he gradually declined to become a more watered-down version of the player that Liverpool initially bought from the Bundesliga, with injuries damaging his exceptional athletic ability, and tactical demands appearing to shackle his originality in possession.

When he departed after his contract expired in 2023, still just 28 years old, he seemed like a shadow of the dynamo that Edwards acquired in 2018. Keïta is now regarded by some sections of supporters as one of Liverpool's worst-ever signings, largely because of his failure to justify his costly transfer. Edwards moved heaven and earth to bring the captain of Guinea to Anfield, but he made just 129 appearances in all competitions – averaging around 26 per season – with many of those involving him being used as a substitute. For the most part, Keïta was a net positive when he was involved, but that was the problem. He simply couldn't get on the pitch often enough to stamp his mark on Klopp's team, unlike a certain full-back who joined the

Reds in the same summer that Edwards agreed his peculiar deal for Keïta.

Robertson was once earmarked by Graham as another one of his gems. The Scottish left-back moved to Anfield around five weeks before Liverpool struck a deal with Keïta's representatives, costing as little as £8m. He was a proper 'Moneyball' signing. Just 23 years old at the time, Robertson was contracted to Hull City, who struggled at the foot of the Premier League. He formed part of a dysfunctional outfit and, because of their failure to compete, Robertson spent most of his time defending and was rarely allowed to venture into the final third. Nevertheless, Liverpool recognised his offensive qualities and believed he would prosper in a different and more favourable environment.

'One of my favourite players is Robertson, our left-back, one of the best left-backs in Europe, and now a European champion of course,' Graham later said. 'His problem was his background as much as anything. He only started playing Premier League football around the age of 22. He was the best young full-back in Britain at the time. He was a strange case of a really attacking full-back playing in a really poor defensive team.' Edwards moved for him after Hull confirmed their relegation by finishing 18th in the table. Players who suffered relegation were generally deemed as not good enough for the big leagues. If they were good enough, they wouldn't have been relegated, right? In Robertson's case, Liverpool spotted an opportunity by appreciating his difficult circumstances alongside his reduced value, with relegated players usually sold for less in the transfer market.

Georginio Wijnaldum and Xherdan Shaqiri also joined the Reds from relegated clubs near the beginning of Klopp's tenure. Signing those players allowed Edwards to exploit an apparent market inefficiency, the kind that John Henry had chased throughout his career. Upon his arrival at Anfield, Robertson transformed and developed into a cult hero of sorts. Klopp's attacking methods – and his charitable midfield department – allowed him to flourish, and his pressing game presented him with a platform to flaunt his relentless running power. Robertson had always been a roadrunner at heart, but his situation at Hull had masked his true capabilities. In the winter of 2022 he registered the 54th assist of his Premier League career, 50 of which had been delivered in a Liverpool shirt, becoming the highest-assisting defender in the competition's history.

Graham's prescriptions didn't always form the heart of Liverpool's transfer moves. His data-driven viewpoint was one of many considered by Edwards and those making expensive recruitment decisions. Peter Moores, who was CEO from 2017 until 2020, was a speaker at the World Football Summit in 2019. The Liverpool-born business executive offered an insight into the inner workings of the club in his talk:

> We look at data. There's a merging of that data with experienced eyes, so the analogue and the digital come together, and a lot of that legacy is the belief that John Henry, Tom Werner and Mike Gordon have in owning the Boston Red Sox. They hadn't won the World Series for 86 years, but applied science and technology to analysing

players and understanding what players need for the Red Sox to create the best chance to win. It is that combination of an experienced eye looking at an athlete combined with data, combined with psychological outputs. We have a sporting director who is akin to a general manager in American sports. He and our scouting staff and analytical staff are the ones who build the squad. Jürgen Klopp as the manager gets the best out of that squad. Together we come together as an entity.

Edwards refrained from signing players solely according to their performances in the data; he said as much in his open letter to supporters in 2021. Liverpool did, however, appreciate and consider the value of data, perhaps more than any other club in the world. 'The concept of "Moneyball", as it was formerly well-known,' said Moores. 'In particular what we embraced was looking at players who fit a certain criteria that the team needed, good value for money, younger and could deliver against what we needed. We apply data, statistics and metrics to our players as well as our scouts. There's no other team in the Premier League and perhaps European football that uses data like we do.' Liverpool's approach to scouting for talent was multifaceted. Graham's input was considered, but his analysis was supported by several other departments, with each contributing to ensure the club's sporting director didn't make a single mistake in the market.

One particular way in which data refined Liverpool's recruitment was through filtering. In 2019, reports emerged in the public domain that suggested Manchester United had assessed 804 right-backs before settling upon Aaron Wan-Bissaka of Crystal Palace for £50m. The price paid for his services was trivial in comparison to the sheer number of players that had been considered for the role. A shortlist of 804 players is not a shortlist. In fact, those reports almost captured how inefficient United's practices seemed to be, rather than offering an insight into how extensive their global network was. Graham's department allowed Liverpool to look far afield without ever having to leave Merseyside. He could flag outliers from his laptop, and on the back of identifying obscure names who seemed to shine, scouts proceeded to have a closer look by delving deeper. The exploration of overlooked markets was a hidden perk attached to his department. He said:

> There's a worldwide free market of football players. The real power of data analysis is when the data set is large. We have detailed data on hundreds of thousands of players, but maybe only five per cent of those would be anywhere near Premier League level. But that's still 5,000 players, which is too big a set of players to scout everyone in depth and in detail. So we can really help that identification process.

Liverpool acquired the services of Takumi Minamino in 2020. The Japanese forward moved from Red Bull Salzburg at the time for a modest £7.25m. He was regularly crowned as a champion of Austria, but he wasn't one of the headline acts in Salzburg. A quiet and introverted character,

Minamino was versatile, offensive, proactive and willing to work for his team-mates, but he was the type of player who would usually go unnoticed. Players from Austria don't tend to move directly to the Premier League, especially to clubs competing at the top of the table, but Liverpool took a chance on him.

Kostas Tsimikas is another player who was purchased from a relatively exotic location. The 24-year-old defender had spent his career performing outside of the very best competitions in Europe. He was contracted to Olympiacos at the time, and had previously spent isolated seasons in the Netherlands and Denmark. Tsimikas stood out in comparison to his peers in Greece. He posed far more of a threat going forward than every other full-back in his homeland, and he was deemed to be a suitable support act for Robertson, who would need to recharge his limitless batteries every now and then. For just £11.75m, Liverpool bought Tsimikas, and whenever Klopp called upon his services to cover for Robertson, the Greek international stepped up. Minamino and Tsimikas weren't superstars, but their transfers allowed Liverpool to fill lesser voids within their squad at a minimum cost. The willingness to think outside the box paid dividends.

Mohamed Salah is perhaps the most obvious of Liverpool's data-fuelled transfers. In 2017, Klopp was still in the process of constructing his new-look attack, having been at the helm for a year and a half, but Philippe Coutinho was toying with the prospect of leaving. He was the best player at Anfield in the eyes of many and had been at the club since the days of Damien Comolli and Brendan Rodgers. Klopp's players had become accustomed to giving the ball to their Brazilian team-mate whenever they encountered difficulties, but it was time to evolve. Barcelona had courted Coutinho's services for some time, and with his sale on the horizon Edwards planned ahead and made an early move for his replacement. Julian Brandt was reported as the man that Klopp wanted. The Bayer Leverkusen prospect was showing signs of becoming a star in his homeland, but Edwards and Graham had other ideas. Salah, according to their analysis, was the man to get. 'He will score goals, trust us,' was the message to Klopp. He was a player who Liverpool had tried to acquire three years earlier, but José Mourinho stepped in and encouraged his club to sign him after Salah scored twice across two Champions League matches against his Chelsea outfit, while representing FC Basel. The narrative surrounding the Egyptian forward was strong when Liverpool's fresh interest resurfaced in 2017. He was regarded as a Premier League flop because of his failed spell at Stamford Bridge, but the label was unfair. 'Salah didn't fail at Chelsea,' said Graham. 'He failed to get on the pitch.'

Mourinho presented Salah with just six starts in the Premier League before he was loaned to Fiorentina 12 months later, and sold to AS Roma six months after that. Liverpool saw through his status as a flop and assessed the level of his performances in Florence and Rome. You didn't need a PhD to recognise that Salah was an output merchant. His basic offensive numbers were enough to grab the attention of even the most amateur analyst. Across two seasons, Salah played 5,196 minutes in the Italian top flight and registered a goal or an assist every 113 minutes. He found the net 29 times from a wide starting position –

without taking a single penalty – while providing the assist for 17 goals scored by his team-mates. The pacey forward was naturally inclined to have an impact on his team's goal difference, and he never missed a match. He was a bona fide star, and he was packed full of end product.

Liverpool saw through the bias surrounding his name and, unlike Rodgers during his time on Merseyside, Klopp was willing to listen to the expert advice of those around him. Edwards agreed to sign Salah for around £34m and, to his surprise, he was able to bring him to the club without having to fend off a single rival bidder. No other club had expressed much of an interest in signing the African forward, which perhaps epitomised the footballing landscape at the time. Statistics were becoming more prominent, but they still seemed to be neglected by the large majority of top clubs, especially those big enough to poach a key player from a club as big as AS Roma.

Once forming part of Klopp's team, Salah ensured that Coutinho wouldn't be missed. He was a perfect fit on the right side of the pitch, cutting inside using his favoured left foot before finding the far corner of the net, with Roberto Firmino creating openings for him through the middle. With Sadio Mané offering the same qualities from the left side, Klopp had a balanced and symmetrical attack with pace and penetration installed either side of the artful Firmino, who went largely unnoticed as Liverpool's puppet master.

In his debut campaign at Anfield, Salah broke the Premier League record for most goals in a single 38-match season, scoring 32 times, ahead of Cristiano Ronaldo, Luis Suárez and Alan Shearer, who each shared the previous record of 31. In that monumental season he became the first player to single-handedly outscore three teams in West Bromwich Albion, Swansea City and Huddersfield Town. Salah won the Premier League's Player of the Month award on three separate occasions in that campaign, which no player had ever done before. He scored 44 goals in all competitions, which is the most that any Liverpool player has ever scored in a debut campaign. Salah later became the first Reds player to score at least 20 goals in three separate Premier League seasons. In 2020/21, he scored 20 away goals in all competitions, with no Liverpool player ever scoring as many in a single campaign. In 2021/22, Salah scored his 100th Premier League goal for Klopp in his 151st appearance, reaching the milestone quicker than any player in the club's history. In late 2023, he became the first player to score or assist in ten consecutive appearances in the Premier League since himself between August and December in 2021. No opposition player except for Salah has ever scored a Premier League hat-trick against Manchester United at Old Trafford. No player has scored more goals for Liverpool in the Champions League than Salah. No African player has scored more goals in Premier League history than Salah. How long have you got?

Every time a Premier League player seemingly does the unthinkable by scoring in a certain number of consecutive matches or reaching a specific landmark in record time, he often finds out that Salah is the only player who has achieved such a feat before him. Yeah, you've done well, but Salah has already done it. The list of records broken by the Egyptian captain after he returned to English shores is almost endless. Of all of the players signed by Liverpool during the FSG era, nobody endorsed their scientific approach more appropriately than the guy who seemed to accumulate numbers in his sleep.

Chapter Ten

Transformers

BUILDING A SQUAD is a lot like solving a jigsaw puzzle in football. The players are the pieces, and they're supposed to come together to form one united and harmonious structure. As each piece is added in the correct place over time, the jigsaw puzzle gets closer to the finished article, but it doesn't take much for things to go wrong. A piece in the wrong place can have a detrimental impact on future moves and how the rest of the puzzle gets constructed. The same is true in football. A squad is always in need of at least one specific piece in order to improve or get closer to completion but, often, clubs identify the wrong missing element before ending up further away from their desired destination. Rather than evolving and making the next step, the opposite happens.

In the summer window of 2021, both Chelsea and Manchester United made similar errors in the transfer market. At Stamford Bridge, Thomas Tuchel had recently won the Champions League in his debut campaign in charge. The Premier League title was next on the agenda for the German coach, who believed his team to be in need of a true striker above all else. A physical presence through the centre was required, who could act as a focal point for others to move around. Tuchel got his wish and landed Romelu Lukaku from Inter Milan for a club-record fee of £97.5m. Although the Belgian international experienced a promising start in London, he shortly fell out of favour at Chelsea due to his apparent lack of compatibility with his team-mates and the system around him. In early 2022, he set a new Premier League record for the fewest touches from a player who had played a full 90 minutes since statistics first started being recorded by Opta in 2003. He amassed just seven touches against Crystal Palace, with one originating from kick-off.

'The data is out there and the data speaks a certain language,' Tuchel later admitted. 'He was not involved in our game, it's sometimes like this with strikers.' As Manchester City and Liverpool accumulated 93 and 92 points that season without using a conventional striker, Chelsea posted 74 points with Lukaku making just 16 starts from a possible 38, and ten appearances from the bench. In hindsight, his transfer wasn't needed, and his impact was more negative than positive. He was loaned back to Inter Milan just 12 months after moving to London, before being loaned to AS Roma one year after that.

At Old Trafford, Ole Gunnar Solskjær's midfield department was widely regarded as the overwhelming weak point of his squad, yet United decided to sanction moves for a centre-back and two attacking players in Raphaël Varane, Jadon Sancho and Cristiano Ronaldo. The latter scored 18 goals in the Premier League, which was twice the amount of every one of his team-mates except for Bruno Fernandes on ten. The prodigal son had returned, aged 37. He was home. The six-time Ballon d'Or winner was the cherry on the cake, but by the end of the season United had finished sixth, with 16 points fewer than in their previous campaign. The goal difference column of the table captured how they were 29 goals worse than in their previous season despite Ronaldo's scoring rate, and Solskjær was sacked less than three months after the Portuguese superstar's glamorous arrival.

The balance of the squad had been disrupted in favour of stardom, nostalgia and sentiment, with United only moving for their golden goose after his name was linked with a possible transfer to the Etihad Stadium as he scrambled to find a way out of Juventus. Solskjær could have used the transfer window to address the obvious voids in his engine room, but United opted for Hollywood names and quickly declined. Ronaldo later fell out with Solskjær's replacement, Erik ten Hag, refusing to be used as a late substitute in a match against Tottenham Hotspur, before being allowed to leave the club by mutual agreement ahead of the 2022 World Cup, having recorded a controversial and unlicensed interview with Piers Morgan. Less than 18 months after his celebrated return to Old Trafford, Ronaldo was representing Al Nassr in Saudi Arabia. 'Bringing Ronaldo back was a decision that was difficult to turn down and I felt we had to take it, but it turned out wrong,' Solskjaer later admitted in an interview with *The Athletic*. 'It felt so right when he signed and the fans felt that at the Newcastle United game, when Old Trafford was rocking.' It was all about feelings and emotions for the Red Devils, with vibes prevailing above all else.

If you conduct the right transfer business, you take one step forward. If you conduct the wrong business, you tend to take two steps back. The Premier League era is packed full of examples of clubs steadily evolving by instalments, before falling off a cliff having identified the wrong department of need to address in the transfer market. As a consequence of Michael Edwards replacing Philippe Coutinho's presence before he had actually left the club – through the acquisition of pacey forward Mohamed Salah – Liverpool were able to view the sale of their gifted Brazilian through a data lens and with a fresh pair of eyes. They raised £142m for his services, and those funds would be reinvested into Jürgen Klopp's squad.

Edwards even managed to insert a unique clause into the terms of the deal with Barcelona, which would force the Catalan giants to pay a premium of £80m in addition to any agreed figure if they wanted to sign another Liverpool player before 2021. After witnessing Coutinho and Luis Suárez both leave Anfield for the Camp Nou – and Javier Mascherano before them – Edwards was intent on stopping Barcelona from continuing to circle around the brightest stars on Merseyside. With over £100m in the bank, Liverpool had cash to throw at their goal difference. As supporters speculated about who would replace Coutinho, even though Salah had already done exactly that, Ian Graham analysed the main weaknesses of Klopp's team. 'Let's say we've got a budget of £50m for transfers this season,' Graham once suggested before explaining Liverpool's methods. 'What is the maximum improvement we could get with that transfer budget?' That same question was applied to Coutinho's sale. How could

Liverpool best improve their goal difference using over £100m, regardless of who had been sold? The answer lay in their defence.

Klopp had prioritised offensive improvement throughout his time at Anfield. As an attacking coach, he needed threatening players to execute his principles, dedicating his early budgets to the likes of Salah, Georginio Wijnaldum, Sadio Mané and Alex Oxlade-Chamberlain. In defence, Liverpool were far less willing to splash the cash, acquiring players such as Joël Matip on a free transfer, Ragnar Klavan for around £4m and Loris Karius for close to £5m. Aside from Andy Robertson, who also cost as little as £8m, Liverpool's defence was desperate for real investment. When Coutinho left in the middle of the 2017/18 campaign, Liverpool had scored the second-most goals in England at the time, all while conceding more than five other teams, including Burnley. Their tendency to concede too often had to be addressed, so replacing Coutinho with yet another attacker simply didn't make any sense, especially with Salah already in the building.

In the same mid-season window that the South American was sold, Liverpool bought Virgil van Dijk for a record-breaking fee. The Dutch centre-back cost £75m. He became the most expensive defender ever, and also became Liverpool's most expensive transfer ever. Edwards gambled by paying such an extortionate figure for a player contracted to Southampton, who were eighth in the Premier League table at the time, but Liverpool were almost certain of his effect on their goal difference. Van Dijk offered effective qualities, although some of them drifted under the radar because of the stylistic nature of Southampton, much like

Robertson's case at Hull. Standing around 6ft 4in tall, he was a colossus and, despite his size and imposing physique, he was quicker than the large majority of strikers. Bigger than everybody else. Faster than everybody else. Stronger than everybody else. All of those subtle edges allowed him to dominate virtually all his opponents in difficult one-on-one situations. He was cool when in possession of the ball, and nothing ever seemed to fluster him. His general calmness allowed him to make optimal decisions when defending, rather than making calamitous errors like some of his predecessors at Anfield. He was skilled at hitting long passes over defences, and his addition wouldn't just help Liverpool's fortunes against the ball, it would have an impact on several departments in both attack and defence.

Assessing centre-backs using numbers is known to be complicated. Data in the world of football primarily revolves around events, at least in public spaces. Tackles are recorded, clearances are recorded, interceptions are recorded, but it was Paolo Maldini who famously suggested that having to make a tackle means a mistake has already been made. Xabi Alonso, who won the Champions League with Liverpool in 2005 and also formed part of historic teams at Real Madrid and Bayern Munich, agrees with the legendary Italian. In an interview with *The Guardian* in 2011, the Spaniard famously stated that he didn't believe tackling was a quality. 'It is a recurso, something you have to resort to, not a characteristic of your game,' he said. 'Tackling is a [last] resort, and you will need it, but it isn't a quality to aspire to, a definition.'

From a numbers perspective, defenders could theoretically perform well against the ball but, as a result of their expert positioning and reading of the game, they could appear quiet and inactive in the data. When it comes to analysing the numbers posted by forward players, the more the better is a general rule of thumb, but the case is far more complex at the opposite end of the pitch. Much of Van Dijk's success when defending stemmed from his power over the decisions made by his opponents. He was able to dictate the choices made by opposition attackers, forcing players to become negative in possession, all without ever touching the ball. Van Dijk famously made 50 appearances for Liverpool in the Premier League from March 2018 to August 2019 without being dribbled past. Any analysis undertaken to determine his level of contribution to a team had to consider far more than standard event data.

Van Dijk would make a valuable difference to Liverpool around set-pieces in particular. He was tall, assertive and one of the league's best at contesting for aerial balls. In the season that Liverpool signed him, he engaged in 119 aerial duels in the Premier League, losing just 23, which left him with a success rate of 80.7 per cent, placing him second in the division. The following season, he placed top by the same numbers. The season after that he placed second to Matip, his Liverpool team-mate, who played fewer minutes. By the end of the 2021/22 campaign, Van Dijk had scored 11 goals in the Premier League for Liverpool, with every one originating from a dead-ball situation. When defending those same scenarios at the opposite end, he was equally as transformative. In the full season before Van Dijk signed, Liverpool conceded 12 Premier League goals from set-pieces, while scoring 13 in attack, resulting in a mediocre goal difference from set-pieces of just +1. In the full season after he signed, 2018/19, Liverpool conceded just eight times while scoring 20 themselves, equating to a healthy goal difference of +12. Van Dijk wasn't solely responsible for the upturn but even when he didn't touch the ball he played his part, acting as a decoy of sorts for Klopp's coaching team to build routines around.

Liverpool could have almost justified much of his price tag based on his impact from set-pieces alone. As a pillar of strength who rarely made a mistake, never gave away goals for free, contributed to attacking moves and bolstered the strength of Klopp's team around set-pieces, Van Dijk transformed Liverpool from contenders to challengers. From good to great. From top four to top two. In 2022, Van Dijk set a new Premier League record. He played his 60th top-flight match for Liverpool at Anfield without experiencing a single loss, recording 52 victories alongside eight draws, which bettered Lee Sharpe's previous record of 59 home matches undefeated for Manchester United. There's an argument to suggest that no signing throughout Klopp's tenure had more of an impact on Liverpool's goal difference than Van Dijk at his peak, although Salah would likely argue otherwise. His prominence explained why Edwards was willing to sanction such an uncharacteristically large transfer fee to land his services. He was expensive, but he would provide a return on the club's investment through the currency of goal difference.

Six months after Van Dijk formed the backbone of Klopp's defence, Liverpool broke yet another transfer record by making Alisson Becker the world's most expensive goalkeeper. Half of the budget from Coutinho's sale still remained, allowing Edwards to further address Liverpool's habit of conceding goals by upgrading their man between the sticks. Alisson cost £65m to secure from AS Roma, which made him almost twice as expensive as Ederson, who held the previous record, having moved from Benfica to Manchester City for £35m just one year earlier. Liverpool were making atypical moves in the transfer market, spending far more than ever before on individual players, but like Van Dijk, Alisson was deemed to be worthy of the outlay. He was labelled as a 'transformational' signing, and Coutinho's departure was paying for his move.

Goalkeepers tend to be undervalued in the footballing world. A team could theoretically get everything right in terms of performance on the pitch, accumulating upwards of 20 shots while allowing their opponents to muster fewer than five, for example, yet all has the potential to be undone by a random moment of substandard goalkeeping. The low-scoring nature of football can punish goalkeepers. An isolated mistake, a lapse in judgement or a poor attempt at making a save can decide a 90-minute clash in an instant. The influence that goalkeepers can have on performances is relatively limited, but their influence on results can be enormous.

In a conversation with *The Athletic* in 2020, Daniel Finkelstein, the columnist behind the Fink Tank, recalled his collaborations with Graham and Decision Technology. 'Ian became the driver of much of our work at the Fink Tank,' he said. 'We were using a language to talk about football that was profoundly important for football itself, and understanding things the game did not understand.

We understood rapidly that goalkeepers were undervalued financially and it is no surprise to me to see £60m goalkeepers now.' Liverpool had suffered at the hands of questionable goalkeeping on countless occasions before Alisson signed. Klopp's players would deliver consistent defensive performances on a regular basis by pressing their opponents into the ground high up the pitch, but their results failed to adequately represent those watertight showings, and much of the disconnect stemmed from their goalkeeping department.

The final of the Champions League in 2017/18 provided a perfect example and, coincidentally, it was the last match that Liverpool played under Klopp before Alisson's luxury purchase was given the green light. The scores were level in Kyiv after 50 minutes against Real Madrid, before Karius accidentally rolled the ball to the feet of Karim Benzema, who opened the scoring. Then 30 minutes later Liverpool conceded their third goal of the match after Gareth Bale hit a swerving shot from 30 yards, which Karius tried to catch but dropped into his own net. Simon Mignolet occupied the Anfield net before him, but the Belgian was equally as susceptible to moments of disaster. Klopp could have fielded the most well-oiled unit of players in the world but, without a competent goalkeeper, results always seemed destined to fluctuate. A coin flip was always involved.

Goalkeepers, like defenders, can be difficult to analyse. They're entirely separate to outfield players and, as a consequence, almost a whole new approach is required to decrypt their contributions. In goal difference terms, their natural means of adding value comes from making saves, although shot-stopping can be as capricious as finishing.

Players can experience hot streaks. Players can experience cold streaks. The most practised way in which to assess goalkeeping using data when Alisson was signed was to apply expected goal – or post-shot expected goals for the initiated – to determine how many times a goalkeeper conceded in comparison to how many goals he should have realistically conceded based on the shots on target that he faced. Assessing those numbers generally allowed analysts to identify which goalkeepers had performed to an above average standard in terms of shot-stopping through their ability to save more than expected.

In 2013, Liverpool bought Mignolet from Sunderland for £9m. He was 25 years old at the time and in the season before his move his saves grabbed the headlines. Having occupied the starting spot for a team who finished 17th in the Premier League, Mignolet's goal was peppered with shots, but his performance against expectation was very strong. According to Opta's goals prevented metric, he posted an overperformance of 15.7 goals that season. No goalkeeper in Premier League history has ever posted higher in a single campaign based on Opta's model, with David de Gea ranking second, having prevented 13.7 goals under José Mourinho in 2017/18. The reasoning behind Liverpool's decision to sign Mignolet back then has always remained under wraps, but the club's recruitment team could have easily been deceived by the data attached to his showings at the time. Upon his arrival on Merseyside, Mignolet displayed moments of good form but struggled with life closer to the summit of the table. He wasn't comfortable with the ball at his feet, he seemed to have a tendency to overthink situations, and he didn't have the skills to dominate one-on-one duels against strikers. He was presented with scenarios that were entirely different to those he was used to facing for Sunderland, with the Black Cats often defending as part of a block in front of their goal.

The year before Liverpool signed Mignolet, Tottenham Hotspur invested in Hugo Lloris, acquiring him to become their new goalkeeper from Lyon for just £11.8m. Four years prior, the Frenchman was on Damien Comolli's radar as he searched for a successor for the ageing Brad Friedel. The Spurs sporting director consulted Decision Technology at the time, with Graham in favour of the transfer after evaluating his numbers. As a 21-year-old goalkeeper, he looked very promising. Four years passed before Spurs completed the transfer, with Lloris eventually becoming captain of the team. While he's always been prone to making spontaneous errors, his general shot-stopping performances have been impressive throughout his career. In fact, from 2017/18 to 2021/22, he prevented 16.3 goals above expectation in the Premier League per Opta's model.

As De Gea excelled on English shores in 2017/18, Alisson did exactly the same in Italy. According to Opta, he prevented 7.4 goals above expectation for Roma in Serie A. StatsBomb's equivalent model painted him in a similar light, placing him above every goalkeeper in Europe's top five leagues, marginally ahead of Atlético Madrid's Jan Oblak and Burnley's Nick Pope. He looked like a superior goalkeeper in the data, but was this another trap? Unlike Mignolet, Alisson didn't just offer shot-stopping strength; he was a natural sweeper who dared to explore the open spaces beyond his six-yard box. Ederson and Marko Dmitrović were the only two goalkeepers across Europe who averaged more defensive actions outside their penalty box than Alisson in his final season in Rome. Being typically Brazilian, he was at home when passing out from the back, and he largely refrained from making spontaneous mistakes that decided results, unlike Mignolet. Even if his goals prevented numbers from 2017/18 were somewhat inflated or unsustainable, Alisson was an obvious upgrade on what Liverpool had. Across his first five seasons at Anfield, he prevented 28.5 goals in the Premier League and Champions League. Liverpool had paid a premium but, with Alisson on board, the team's goal difference was bound to improve. Klopp had acquired a goalkeeper who would do him favours for once, unlike Mignolet, Karius and even Roman Weidenfeller, particularly in his final season at Borussia Dortmund. His purchase ensured that opponents would have to work for their goals against Liverpool, freebies were no longer available.

In Alisson's first campaign on Merseyside, Liverpool conceded the fewest goals in Europe's top five leagues on 22, which was 16 fewer than in their previous season. Klopp's men won the Champions League and lost just one Premier League match from a possible 38. Football is a team game, but the cliché line that no team can ever win anything meaningful without a proper goalkeeper might be one of the few pieces of conventional wisdom to bear fruit. In Van Dijk and Alisson, Liverpool bought a pair of genuine transformers with their money in the bank. Elements of traditional scouting formed an essential part of the recruitment process to ensure the blind spots of the past were studied this time around, but without the application of data to the question of how to improve, the direction of Liverpool's squad building could have easily followed a very different path. Not only did Graham's analysis help determine the weakest areas of Klopp's squad in goal difference terms, but his work justified the exceptional costs attached to signing both players. They were expensive, but they were worth it, and Liverpool were able to prove that with scientific evidence rather than rudimentary opinions like those that guided the business conducted by Manchester United and Chelsea.

Chapter Eleven

Pitch Control

'FOOTBALL IS too dynamic,' said John Henry in 2011, one year after becoming owner of Liverpool. While still getting to grips with the sport and reading *Soccernomics* by Simon Kuper and Stefan Szymanski in his spare time, his words captured one of the main reasons why analysis and scouting for players in football must incorporate far more than basic data. The game is simply too continuous, free-flowing and random to be analysed with any degree of certainty using event data alone. The unpredictable nature of the sport perhaps offers an insight into why half of transfers tend to fail, according to Ian Graham.

In 2021, the Cambridge physicist analysed every transfer that had cost over €10m in the Premier League dating back to the January window of 2010 and found that new signings generally started around just 50 per cent of matches across the two seasons following their moves. He outlined seven key reasons behind why players tend to fail once changing clubs, with some more controllable than others. The basic causes listed by Graham were as follows:

- a current player is better than the new player
- the new player is not as good as first thought
- the new player doesn't fit the style of the team
- the new player is played out of position
- the manager doesn't rate the new player
- the new player has fitness issues
- the new player has personal issues

Data and analytics, according to his perspective, has significant power over the first three of those concerns, with Liverpool eager to improve upon the generic 50 per cent hit rate in the transfer market. The bleak success rate wasn't good enough, and part of Graham's remit was to ensure that Liverpool minimised the level of risk attached to buying new players. He had lots of isolated metrics at his disposal from shots to passes to clearances and everything in between, but he needed to find a way of incorporating the dynamic and fluid complexity of football that Henry had referenced. Knowing that a player had made a forward pass wasn't enough, Liverpool wanted context. They wanted the full picture. They wished to gather information surrounding the locations of every player on the pitch when that forward pass was made, and how that pass truly influenced proceedings in a positive or negative way. 'When we look through the lens of the data, it's not a perfect lens, it's a kind of smeared out view because you don't see all of the details about exactly how much pressure this player was under or exactly where the defenders were,' said Graham in 2019.

The appointment of Will Spearman as a lead data scientist in 2018 would be central to how Liverpool attempted to solve – or at least partially solve – the problem at hand. He arrived on Merseyside with quite a reputation. The American was another PhD holder, this time from Harvard University. Spearman had even worked at the European Organisation for Nuclear Research, where he helped with the discovery of the Higgs boson particle. Before his start at Liverpool, Spearman entered the sports industry through Hudl, a US-based company that has collaborated with over 200,000 teams across more than 40 different sports by 'elevating their performance with video and analytics', according to their website, also acquiring popular scouting tool Wyscout in 2019. While at Hudl in 2016, Spearman and his colleagues explored what tracking data had to offer. In simple terms, tracking data consists of nothing more than positional coordinates, and it was actually on the scene before event data, but nobody really knew what to do with it. Premier League stadiums are fitted with a series of cameras, and those cameras record the positions of the players and the ball at 25 frames per second for the entirety of a match. The resulting product is a package of more than a million data points per match for scientists to decrypt.

While at Hudl, Spearman demonstrated a knack for unearthing some of the hidden powers of tracking data, which had previously been used to assess physical performance above all else, covering common Prozone elements such as top speed, sprints and distance covered. Spearman's creation was a concept that he named 'pitch control', which aimed to quantify the control of space in football. Pitch control almost appeared like a classic Football Manager match engine when in action, showing the locations of every player on the pitch – and the ball – using a bird's eye view from above. Space controlled by Liverpool shone red as the match progressed, space controlled by the opposition shone blue, and space that was uncertain remained white. Spearman's interactive model constantly changed according to the players and the location of the ball, so it could show how much of the pitch Liverpool controlled at any given moment while visualising how certain movements or passes influenced proceedings positively or negatively.

Rather than understanding that Jordan Henderson had made a forward pass on the hour mark and nothing more, Spearman's work allowed Liverpool to determine whether his pass bypassed any opponents. Did Henderson's pass break the lines of the opposition, was it the most advantageous decision that he could have made at the time, and how often does he tend to make the most optimal choice when in possession? All those types of insights were gathered by harvesting what tracking data was hiding under the bonnet. Liverpool could gauge which types of passes were generally valued as dangerous, which players usually increased or decreased their team's probabilities of scoring with their contributions, and what the most optimal pass was in any given scenario. With Henderson in possession, Spearman's pitch control model could determine which spaces of the pitch his team-mates would technically be able to access before their opponents, based on a mathematical combination of the distance of each player to the ball, the time each player takes to cover specific distances – given that players who are quicker than average can travel at a faster rate – and further factors.

The importance of speed in relation to controlling the pitch is curious considering Liverpool have showcased a clear preference for targeting players in the transfer market who possess pace, almost regardless of their role on the pitch. An obvious tactic regardless of any scientific insights, one could argue, but in Virgil van Dijk, for example, Klopp acquired an elite centre-back who had remarkable speed on his side. When required to control open spaces on the defensive side of the game, often without support, it seemed to be easier for him to sweep up loose passes and through balls in comparison to some of his less mobile peers, with Liverpool consequently able to commit more players forward in attack, knowing that Van Dijk could cope as a lone ranger at the back. Ibrahima Konaté was signed from RB Leipzig in 2021 as a future partner for the Dutchman, and he was another physical defender who was rapid across the ground despite his size, standing around 6ft 4in tall. Further forward, Liverpool demonstrated an obsession for signing attackers who were quick enough to pose a threat in behind defences, such as Sadio Mané, Mohamed Salah, Diogo Jota, Luis Díaz and Darwin Núñez. All over the park, perhaps with the exception of a select few players, Liverpool placed a great emphasis on speed and mobility when scouting for talent.

Graham has also described the perks of tracking data when opening up about Liverpool's methods. 'We get data on every ball touched by every player in every game, where it was on the pitch, and what happened next,' he said. 'We can see where all of the players are at 25 frames per second. It's done with optical tracking, the same technology that's used for missile tracking originally. It's much easier to

track a person than a missile, they travel a little slower.'
In 2019, Tim Waskett featured as a guest speaker in the annual Royal Institution Christmas Lectures. An indie games developer in his spare time, Waskett formed part of Graham's research team alongside Spearman and Dafydd Steele, as well as Mark Howlett and Mark Stevenson. The latter two previously worked in Liverpool's technology department before Graham integrated them into his data science team. 'They are responsible for the technology side of it, maintaining the database for us, building our research website and so on,' he said. 'They do all the tech stuff and that lets the four of us focus on the data science part of it.'

In Waskett's short presentation, the PhD holder in X-ray astronomy showed how pitch control was used to help with recruitment at Liverpool:

> The primary currency that every game is based on is goals. It's our job to turn every action on the pitch – every pass, every throw-in, every tackle, every shot – into a goal probability. For every game, we get approximately 2,000 ball touch events and the positions of the players who make those touches. What that doesn't tell you is where all of the other players are on the pitch at that moment, but for Premier League games we also get tracking data. This data can be used to give us a goal value for every position and every player on the pitch at any given time.

Waskett showed an animated visualisation of Spearman's pitch control model in action during his talk, with

Trent Alexander-Arnold in possession of the ball in his own half of the pitch. The animation was paused, and '1.3 per cent EPV' emerged in the top left corner. EPV stood for expected possession value. '1.3 per cent is the probability that a goal will be scored within the next 15 seconds,' Waskett explained. As the animation continued, Alexander-Arnold proceeded to carry the ball from his own half towards the edge of the opposition penalty box, boosting his team's 1.3 per cent to 7.2 per cent. Throughout the clip, red spaces emerged in different parts of the pitch, highlighting the areas that Liverpool could access before their opponents and showing where Alexander-Arnold should consider passing the ball if he wanted to make an optimal decision. 'The main way we use this is to evaluate player performance after the game,' Waskett said. 'With tracking data, we can see all of the players at the same time, and analyse all of the players within the Premier League. It gives us some really good information on which players are doing well, and who we might be able to sign in the future.'

Several leagues across Europe sourced their own official tracking data through companies such as STATSPerform, InStat, ChyronHego and Second Spectrum. The Premier League signed a three-year deal with the latter in 2019. They were acquired by Genius Sports in 2021. However, Liverpool naturally wanted their scouting network to expand beyond England. Access to data associated with Premier League football was valuable, but what about the rest of Europe? Graham had a problem to navigate, as the tracking data attached to other major leagues remained confidential for the clubs involved.

Real Madrid had access to La Liga numbers, Juventus had access to Serie A numbers, Bayern Munich had access to Bundesliga numbers, and so on.

To overcome the hurdle, Graham contacted the services of SkillCorner in 2018. At the time, the French start-up was providing betting companies with live animations, showing the locations of the players and the ball during football matches. Rather than using their own cameras like an official in-stadium provider, SkillCorner used broadcast footage and artificial intelligence (AI) to track the movements of players and the ball, relying on their partnership with the video scouting platform that is now under Hudl's umbrella, Wyscout. The creation, again, was very Football Manager in appearance, almost like Spearman's work, with counters moving around the pitch having been visualised from above.

Hugo Bordigoni, co-founder of the company, opened up about Graham's initial interest in an interview with Training Ground Guru in 2020. After seeing their data visualisations, the Welshman wanted to know more, said Bordigoni. 'If you're doing this using broadcast footage, this could be interesting for us in player recruitment,' Graham told him. Liverpool dedicated a year to helping SkillCorner evolve their product into a performance-related tool, before signing a contract with them. 'Liverpool were happy with the tracking data they got for the Premier League and Champions League, but if they wanted to scout players in France, Spain, Germany and beyond, they couldn't access the data from those countries,' said Bordigoni. By 2022, SkillCorner were covering more than 45 competitions worldwide, and their product delivered up to 98 per cent accuracy in comparison to in-stadium official tracking systems. Bordigoni said:

> If there was a pass at 3 minutes 42 in a particular match, they can look at the tracking data at this exact frame and say: 'There was this pressing on the player, on the receiver, these were the options he had.' Not a lot of clubs are staffed like Liverpool to handle large amounts of data. They do the modelling on their own. It is not really interesting to know that a player completed 90 passes during a match, but with our data you can assess every pass, and whether there was a better option than the one the player took.

The combination of event data and tracking data added an extra layer to Liverpool's scouting practices. Graham's department was able to distinguish how the actions of a player impacted proceedings strictly in terms of goal difference, with players who generally increased their team's probabilities of scoring, or not conceding, deemed as attractive. Liverpool could identify who was a net positive and who was a net negative by attaining an overall value to all their actions during a match.

In 2020, Thiago Alcântara made the surprise move to Merseyside from Bayern Munich. Numbers weren't required to determine his world-class status as a player, having won a plethora of honours throughout his illustrious career. The Italian-born midfielder ended up effectively replacing Georginio Wijnaldum in Jürgen Klopp's 4-3-3 system, after the reliable Dutchman was allowed to run down his contract, to the surprise of many supporters who hoped he would stay. Wijnaldum and Thiago were the same age and they both offered a similar degree of control and ball retention when in possession, but one was far more incisive and dangerous with his passing than the other. He rarely lost the ball but, crucially, he always added value. Unlike Wijnaldum, who would score occasional goals but refrain from taking risks with his passing, Thiago had a knack for progressing the play and finding his team-mates in the most valuable areas of the pitch. From a pitch control perspective, he was a master at getting the ball into the red spaces and increasing his team's probabilities of scoring with his actions, and all without ever giving the ball away. Graham said:

> The thing I'm really obsessed about is the risk/reward pay-off of passes. Some of the best passers in the game have some of the lowest pass completion percentages, and that's because the risk/reward pay-off is very, very skewed in football. It's very easy to massage statistics and get a high pass completion percentage by playing very conservative passes which do nothing for your team's chances of scoring a goal. The passes I really love are those which go behind the opposition defence and take four or five defenders out of the game. Those passes are really hard to make, but someone who gets those passes correct half the time would be a world-class attacking midfielder.

Thiago was unique in the sense that he was a low-risk but high-reward player in that context, and by using him to replace Wijnaldum, Liverpool essentially became more threatening in attack without losing much strength on the defensive end. 'We are always searching for new weapons,' said Pep Lijnders, Klopp's assistant, in 2022. 'We are always searching for new dynamics. Basically, we want to create the last pass from everywhere, and that should even be a centre-half. Even Alisson Becker.' As Klopp's squad evolved over time, he began to benefit from offensive players in every position. Through the merging of event data with tracking data, Liverpool were able to put a number on space and the threats posed by different players across all their actions, while also exploring the impact of off-ball runs made by players.

The stars who do a lot in possession of the ball have always shone in the numbers, whereas those who use their movement to offer value have always been less inclined to assume the spotlight. Frank Lampard, for example, received constant praise for his ability to find the net and his knack for being in the right place at the right time during his days as a player for Chelsea, as did Dele Alli during his prime at Tottenham Hotspur, but they didn't receive quite as much attention for the quality of their off-ball runs, simply because it's much harder to praise what you cannot quantify. 'When you play a match, players have the ball for three minutes on average,' said Dutch legend Johan Cruyff. 'So the most important thing is what you do during those 87 minutes when you do not have the ball. That is what determines whether you are a good player or not.' The Barcelona and Ajax icon could be right, but it's only since the secrets of tracking data have truly emerged that players are beginning to shine based on their actions without the ball.

At the start of the 2022/23 Premier League campaign, Chelsea's new striker, Nicolas Jackson, was receiving criticism for failing to score in his team's opening two matches of the season against Liverpool and West Ham United. In response to the negativity surrounding his showings, Sky Sports shared a graphic on *The Football Show* highlighting that Jackson had posted more pressures, total runs and runs in the penalty box than any other Chelsea player. There's a debate as to whether those numbers provided any degree of real value considering just two matches had been played at the time but, nevertheless, it was evidence that tracking data was beginning to make an impact in the public space, roughly seven years after Spearman first started to work on his pitch control concept at Hudl. As football continues to evolve, players seem destined to be credited more and more for their off-ball runs, whereas those same players would have previously drifted beneath the surface as unsung heroes. Tracking data is trending now more than ever before, but Liverpool were ahead of the curve, which explains why prominent figures from other sports have sought inspiration from the scientists on Merseyside.

Eddie Jones, who was head coach of the England rugby team for seven years from 2015 until 2022, praised Liverpool's data science department. As he began to broaden his horizons by exploring the inner workings of football during lockdown, he eventually met up with Graham to find out more about how the Reds measured off-ball movements, having also read *Believe Us*, a book about how Liverpool conquered the Premier League, by Melissa Reddy. Jones started to collect data on the back of the meeting, with England employing three members of staff dedicated to that area of expertise. Jones said:

> We had a great meeting with the Liverpool analyst, that's one area they're in. We're starting to develop our own database that can measure work off the ball. That's so important, transitional parts, it's a pretty exciting area for us. [Liverpool], and I think most football sides, are very advanced in being able to measure the movement of the players off the ball. If you look at any [rugby] stats that you get, they are only concerned with information on the ball. We're in the nursery now, whereas Liverpool are doing their PhD at Oxford University. We've got a fair way to go.

By employing Spearman and investing in the dormant potential of tracking data, the Reds gained a clearer picture of what was happening on the pitch before the rest of the world caught up.

Chapter Twelve

Playing Chess with Loaded Dice

BEFORE TAKING to the stage to conduct his talk at the Royal Institution Christmas Lectures in 2019, Tim Waskett was introduced by presenter Hannah Fry as the man whose job it was to make Liverpool 'as lucky as possible' on the pitch.

Football can be wild and chaotic, but the overall objective according to Peter Krawietz, Jürgen Klopp's long-time assistant and best man at his wedding, is to control as many elements as realistically possible. 'The point of coaching is to try to make football – a game based on many random events – less random, to force your luck in a sense,' he said. 'Football is like chess, but with dice. Every coach spends an incredible amount of time pondering about all the different factors: the opponent, weather and so on, knowing full well that total control of the ball is unattainable.' Indeed, 100 per cent control is an unrealistic utopia that's never truly realised in football, although efforts can still be made to repeatedly manage the impact of randomness on results. Some tactical choices perhaps side with probability more than others.

When Klopp first arrived on English shores, he was known for his relatively radical playing style. The German once likened his brand of football to heavy metal music, because it was packed full of emotion, energy and entertainment. He was able to coach his players to thrive more than normal when they were surrounded by apparent anarchy on the pitch, but it wasn't enough to deliver success in the Premier League. A greater degree of control had to be integrated for Liverpool to become as consistent as their fellow title rivals, and once they reached the top they had to keep on getting better as a means of staying there. Klopp had to find ways of making improvements and minimising the element of chance, and after being in charge for several years he was presented with the necessary security in his job to begin exploring subtle edges on the training ground. Ian Graham said:

> Jürgen is very open and receptive to our area. In terms of our week-to-week relationship, I don't have very much interaction with him, but that's not a bad thing because he knows the analysis we do and how it feeds into the various reports and the weekly work that he and his team do. Just the fact that he is open to it and intuitively understands the numbers is enough. And if there is anything in particular that needs addressing, we're there for the coaches. We've done one-off bespoke pieces of work where they're concerned about a particular area of play or want to know something about travel before a game and whether that affects performance. They're

aware that we can help out with stuff and give an opinion on it, which is great. Jürgen is really open to it and understands it.

Graham and his team of scientists never directly interacted with players, but their findings could be filtered through the fabric of the club behind the scenes, with analysts such as Harrison Kingston, who left his role in 2020, Mark Leyland, who joined Newcastle United in late 2021 and then City Football Group in 2023, James French and opposition scout Greg Mathieson bridging the gap to the likes of Klopp and Pep Lijnders, who are eventually presented with the opportunity to put new knowledge into practice on the training ground. 'I'm being generous here, but we can come up with some tactical innovations that can get our team around five more points per season,' Graham said. 'Unfortunately your opponents will work out your tactical innovation before too long and you'll have to do a whole new set of work next season.'

Although the presence of data continues to grow in the sport in comparison to previous decades, the expansion predominantly lies in recruitment, fitness and match analysis rather than tactics and coaching. Few clubs manage to establish the required stability on the training ground to explore the true potential of optimised tactics. With Klopp's position virtually untouchable at Anfield and Graham's team of PhDs harvesting a wealth of valuable insights from data, Liverpool were able to apply numbers to address matters to do with strategy on the pitch, rather than constantly relying on squad turnover and the transfer market to foster change.

Perhaps the most prominent analytics finding relates to shot locations. Expected goals is regarded as the flagship metric in the space. It has taught the football world a very basic lesson: shots closer to goal are converted more often than shots from far out. Nothing new, common sense, but things tend to sink in a little more when there's scientific evidence to support definitive conclusions. As a very generic guideline, around just one per cent to ten per cent of attempts from outside the penalty box result in goals based on the historical outcomes of hundreds of thousands of shots. Inside the penalty box, around 10 per cent to 40 per cent of attempts are converted, and in the six-yard box efforts are scored above 40 per cent of the time. A wide variety of different factors can determine the sophistication of different expected goals models – from the body part used to shoot to the positioning of the goalkeeper, to how much of the goal face is blocked by defenders – but overall, the basic template of where on the pitch players should decide to shoot is clear for those who want to know.

Despite such intelligence, almost 48 per cent of Manchester United's shots in the Premier League in 2019/20 originated from outside the box. Based on the decisions made by their competitors, Liverpool had a real opportunity to begin using probability to shape aspects of their approach. In 2017/18, the average distance from goal of a Liverpool shot in the Premier League was 17.1 yards. The distance dropped to 16.3 yards the following season, and 16.1 yards the season after. In 2020/21, Liverpool encountered a whole host of injury issues that crippled the spine of the team and their average shot distance marginally rose to 16.2 yards, before dropping again to 15.9 yards in the following campaign. Over time, Klopp's men were becoming more and more efficient, with the trio of Roberto Firmino, Sadio Mané and Mohamed Salah growing accustomed to playing together.

In an interview with Tom Worville for *The Athletic* in 2021, Alex Oxlade-Chamberlain showed a clear understanding of the probabilities attached to certain shot locations. 'The biggest one for me is expected positions to score,' he said. After being shown a clip of his famous long-range goal against Manchester City from the 2017/18 campaign, Oxlade-Chamberlain touched on the downsides attached to his attempt. 'It's not a very high percentage of scoring from there. Last season, I think I scored eight goals, four of them from outside of the box. You're going to have to do well to replicate that every year.' The logic is as basic as it gets, but because of the constant upheaval in the footballing world – on and off the pitch – teams just don't get much of an opportunity to properly refine their shooting habits over time.

On the defensive side of the game, Liverpool appeared to use the same straightforward understanding of shot locations to dictate their behaviour. If attempts from close to goal are generally good and attempts from far out are generally bad, encouraging your opponents to do the latter is a sensible but rarely deliberate tactic. In 2022, Chris Summersell presented a case to suggest that Liverpool were breaking a sacred defensive code by consciously opting against blocking shots from distance. The coach and recruitment analyst produced an article that detailed how Liverpool's defenders almost enticed their opponents into shooting from poor locations. Rather than getting in the way of those shots in a conventional manner, Summersell noticed how Klopp's players instead seemed to do the opposite, consequently presenting their goalkeeper, Alisson Becker, with a clear line of vision to make comfortable saves. In his analysis, Summersell found that pressure on shooters against Liverpool generally originated from Klopp's midfielders coming from behind or from the sides, instead of players who would directly disrupt Alisson's view, and defenders actively tried to make themselves small rather than spreading out wide or diving to make blocks. When the article was released, Liverpool had played 29 matches in the Premier League that season and Klopp's players had blocked just 15 per cent of opposition shots from outside the box, which was the lowest percentage in the division by some margin. Next was Brentford on 26 per cent, followed by Manchester City on 28 per cent. The season before, even despite the serious injury crisis at Anfield, Liverpool again placed at the bottom of the division, blocking 29 per cent of opposition efforts from outside the box.

Around 76 per cent of penalties are converted according to expected goals. Rewarding players who are fouled inside the penalty box with such gifts doesn't make much sense as a law of the game, especially considering that if those players were allowed to shoot rather than being fouled, their shots would have likely been worth far less. Given such information, it's reasonable to suggest that attempting to regain the ball by making tackles in the penalty box simply isn't worth the risk. Instead, perhaps blocking shots is more practical in those situations. In

2021/22, Liverpool didn't give away a single penalty across 38 Premier League matches, placing them bottom of the division for penalties faced. In 2019/20, they faced just one, ranking them joint-bottom of the league. The season before, Liverpool again placed bottom of the table, having faced just one. In all of those campaigns, Klopp managed to deliver over 90 points in the Premier League, with Alex Ferguson, who had 21 attempts during his illustrious career at Manchester United, and Pep Guardiola being the only two others to have achieved such a feat in England's top flight. It's curious that when the Reds suffered from their injury crisis in 2020/21 – particularly in the centre of their defence – they gave away eight penalties, with only five teams facing more. The straightforward tactic is so obvious that it shouldn't even have to be mentioned, but, whether it was intentional or not, the removal of opposition penalties from the flavoursome cocktail that's football naturally allowed Liverpool to gain a greater hold over their results.

We live in clichés in patterned behaviour, with sameness often painted as tradition. Players are regularly encouraged to shoot from long range by supporters in stadiums, despite the low probabilities attached to those efforts resulting in goals. Throughout the early stages of their careers, players are instructed by professional coaches to make tackles and block shots regardless of the defensive scenario, which again doesn't wholly add up upon reflection of the evidence. Speaking at Sloan in 2019, Daryl Morey explained how badly teams can get it wrong on the training ground, using basketball as an example. 'When the 3-point line first came in, basketball coaches were actively coaching against it,' he said. 'We now know that was not only wrong, but it was 10 to 15 wins wrong. Catastrophically wrong.' Liverpool, in keeping with a recurring theme on Merseyside, seemed to challenge conventional wisdom and do their own thing when assessing some of the unwritten rules of football, relating to how to attack and how to defend.

They did the same when Klopp decided to appoint the Premier League's first-ever throw-in coach in 2018. The decision was met with ridicule at the time but in Thomas Grønnemark, Liverpool contracted the services of an expert who would add value around a previously untouched element of the sport. Steve Nicol, regarded as one of the best defenders to ever play for Liverpool, mocked the appointment during his punditry duties for ESPN. 'Are you telling me that Klopp and his coaches can't work out throw-ins? Yes this guy can make you throw longer or faster, but don't tell me he's doing anything that we weren't trying to do 30 years ago.' The appointment was a popular topic among panellists, although few credited Liverpool for thinking differently. 'I want to be the first kick-off coach,' joked Andy Gray during beIN Sports coverage of the Premier League. Nevertheless, Liverpool pushed forward. 'I have brought Thomas in to help us improve our throw-ins, because I think it is our biggest weakness,' Klopp told his players.

The average football match consists of around 40 to 50 throw-ins, and Grønnemark found that teams end up losing the ball on more than 50 per cent of the occasions their players received throw-ins under pressure. When Klopp first contacted Grønnemark, his primary concern was how often his players lost possession from those situations. That season, the statistics for throw-ins under pressure suggested Liverpool were the third-worst in the Premier League with a success rate of just 45.4 per cent. One season later, Liverpool's retention dramatically improved, with their success rate of 68.4 per cent ranking them as the second-best in Europe behind only FC Midtjylland, who had also worked with Grønnemark. The Dane, who once set a world-record long throw, appreciated the uniqueness of his role at the club. 'Ninety-nine per cent of the professional players and coaches I'm in contact with have never practised throw-ins,' he told *The Guardian* in 2020.

Liverpool's ability to control their environment on the pitch was marginally strengthened by Grønnemark. In fact, the extent to which Liverpool's ways were shaped by Will Spearman and the findings of pitch control is anybody's guess. For obvious reasons that will primarily remain as a secret, although several aspects of Liverpool's original tactical approach could have theoretically stemmed from understanding how to control and maximise different spaces on the pitch. Even the behavioural traits of Alisson could technically coincide with pitch control. The Brazilian goalkeeper is known for taking up daring positions far from his own goal whenever Liverpool have possession secured further up the pitch, allowing him to sweep up through balls around his own defensive third whenever danger arises. His tendency to vacate his own penalty box helps Liverpool's capacity to own space on the pitch, especially in comparison to goalkeepers who remain glued to their six-yard box at all times.

Spearman produced a paper in 2017, titled 'Physics-Based Modeling of Pass Probabilities in Soccer', in which he attempted to create a model that assessed ball control. His work involved analysing how long it takes any given player to control the ball, which allowed for the creation of new metrics to judge the skill of receivers and defenders. In Spearman's paper, he referenced passing value and receiving/interception efficiency as two examples of innovative metrics that could be derived from his model. Klopp and his analysts were able to apply his work in a tactical sense, identifying pressing 'victims' before matches to determine which opposition player was best to target, with the opponent who took the longest to control the ball deemed as most exploitable. The tactic of focusing on a weak opponent or 'victim' was nothing new for the sport, but using Spearman's work, Liverpool were able to scientifically determine the players who struggled with the ball, rather than relying on the eyes and opinions of a scout or analyst.

It's even possible that Trent Alexander-Arnold's tendency to switch the play from right to left was a by-product of Spearman's work. As Liverpool's right-back, the Scouse defender tends to benefit from more time and space to make an informed decision than most of his teammates. Rio Ferdinand once asked Alexander-Arnold about the quirk on BT Sport. 'I feel as though it's just so effective. If it happens against us, it's 40 to 50 yards of running to get to the other side,' he said. 'Everything shifts, the defenders don't know where things are going. I always think about what I don't want to play against. More people are open, the pitch is bigger, it changes the whole picture.' For three seasons running from 2019/20 to 2021/22, Alexander-Arnold placed top of the Premier League for total switches, with those defined as passes that travel more than 40 yards of the width of the pitch. From left-back, Andy Robertson also posted more than average, although without hitting the same figures as his right-sided team-mate.

Alexander-Arnold is no stranger to learning about optimised decision-making. From a youthful age, he has been exposed to alternative ways in which to improve as a player. In his book, *Intensity*, Lijnders described Alexander-Arnold as the 'epitome of a successful training and coaching process with a young talent'. When he was aged 22, Red Bull released *Trent's Vision*, a short 40-minute movie that saw the Liverpool full-back team up with Daniel Laby, an experienced ophthalmologist. The sports vision expert had worked with numerous MLB teams during his acclaimed career, including his role as a consultant for the Boston Red Sox. 'I started before *Moneyball*,' he told Sky Sports in an interview. 'We have passed through that period of change and we have definitely seen an uptick in interest in what we do, based on this interest in statistics and data-driven selection. Clubs are bringing data scientists into the front office and looking at ways to leverage the technology.' Laby explored ways to enhance Alexander-Arnold's ability to see different elements of the game. He was set numerous personal challenges, some of which were completed on a laptop, whereas others required him to wear a three-dimensional virtual reality headset. 'The eye is a small piece of sports vision. The much larger piece is what happens in the brain,' said Laby.

Indeed, in the summer of 2021, Klopp welcomed Neuro11 to Liverpool's pre-season training camp in Evian. By introducing Niklas Häusler and Patrick Häntschke, co-founders of the German neuroscience company, Liverpool embraced brain power as a means of getting ahead, particularly around set-pieces. 'They are a fixed part of our coaching staff. Everything gets measured, it's incredibly interesting,' said Klopp. 'Penalties are the most obvious thing [they work on], but it's about all set-pieces: corners, free kicks, direct free kicks, crosses and all these kinds of things.' The players who were the most involved with those situations at Liverpool, such as Alexander-Arnold, were given extra sessions with Neuro11 to improve their product on the pitch. The experimental work of Häusler and Häntschke resulted in the pair spending time at Liverpool's training ground in Kirkby during the season.

Set-pieces are being emphasised more and more in the sport. In 2019/20, Liverpool began to demonstrate a preference for out-swinging corners ahead of short, straight or in-swinging alternatives. Klopp's team amassed 122 out-swingers in the Premier League in that season, which was more than double their total of 60 in-swingers and placed them top of the division, ahead of Leicester City on 106 and Chelsea on 86. In the following season, Liverpool again ranked top with 131 out-swingers, while posting just 52 in-swingers, which placed them bottom.

The preference was glaring, but it wasn't until the 2021/22 campaign that people began to truly consider Liverpool's decisions around corners as a thing. They accumulated 204 out-swingers, again placing them top of the Premier League, compared to just 46 in-swingers. Southampton ranked second with 106 out-swingers, followed by Chelsea with 99. In fact, no team from across Europe's big five leagues came close to Liverpool's total, with Inter Milan boasting the second-highest number of out-swingers on 132, followed by Sevilla on 125. Naturally, Liverpool never divulged the reasons behind their selection but, again, numbers could be behind it.

A Stats Perform research paper titled 'Mythbusting Set-Pieces in Soccer' was published in 2018, co-authored by Paul Power, Jennifer Hobbs, Hector Ruiz, Xinyu Wei and Patrick Lucey. The study was based on three seasons of Premier League data, and involved a sample of 12,000 corners. One of the findings suggested that in-swinging corners have a 18.6 per cent chance of leading to a shot compared to 20.9 per cent for out-swinging deliveries. StatsBomb also had a look at the subject, analysing corner types across Europe's big five leagues in 2019/20. Their research found that in-swinging corners are less successful when it comes to finding team-mates. They're completed 30 per cent of the time compared to out-swingers, which are completed 42 per cent of the time. While in-swingers generally prove to be more dangerous when successful – given the nature of how the ball travels towards the goal rather than away from it – they also tend to be harder to get right.

The true extent to which Liverpool allowed data to shape the way in which they played remains to be seen, such is the nature of gaining a secret edge in sport, but there's enough evidence to suggest that Klopp and his coaching staff appreciated how the element of chance could be manipulated. In the future, perhaps optimised tactics will become commonplace. The next generation of footballers could evolve from an early age with an entirely different perspective than their ancestors. Maybe allowing opponents to shoot from distance, within reason, will become the norm. Maybe every team will employ a dedicated throw-in coach. Until then, the most cutting-edge teams who are willing to challenge the status quo will continue to reap the rewards of innovative thinking.

Chapter Thirteen
A Different Type of Arms Race

AFTER IAN Graham became Liverpool's director of research in 2012, Manchester United decided to bide their time before sourcing their own version of the Welshman. Days passed at Old Trafford. Weeks followed. Months passed. Years passed. It wasn't until the end of 2021, nine years later, that Liverpool's historic rivals appointed an equivalent version of Graham, naming Dominic Jordan as their first-ever director of data science. The year that Graham was appointed at Anfield, Manchester City won their first Premier League title under Roberto Mancini, with a 23-year-old version of Sergio Agüero going down in history for his 94th-minute 'moment in time' against Queens Park Rangers. London hosted the Olympic Games, Snapchat had just been created around 12 months earlier and, given that it was 2012, some people expected the world to end.

Upon Jordan's appointment, United didn't have a single data scientist on the football side of their business. He had to start from scratch, much like Graham did, although beginning his work around a decade behind his biggest competitors. Jordan didn't have a background in football. He was an avid United supporter but his previous role was in the fashion industry, having worked as director of data science and analytics at N Brown Group, who owned the likes of Jacamo, Simply Be and JD Williams. Jordan studied mathematics at the University of Cambridge and had a background in geospatial analytics. He said:

> My job will be to build a team of data scientists and analysts who will gather, clean and combine data from all kinds of sources to help the true experts make effective decisions with more confidence. There is so much potential for data science to benefit the club, from assisting with player recruitment, automatically analysing patterns of play right through to using computer vision to extract information from video feeds in real time.

United already used data to analyse performances, opponents and recruitment targets, according to football director John Murtough, who made the appointment. 'When I arrived, there was very little in terms of anyone doing anything with data in any sort of systematic way,' said Graham, but that certainly wasn't the case for Jordan in Manchester.

Liverpool stole a march on United, as did Tottenham Hotspur through their innovative early bond with Decision Technology. In fact, not every club was as slow as United to wake up to the power of data. In 2012, Arsenal made the surprise decision to purchase StatDNA for around

£2.1m. Arsène Wenger, being the visionary that he was, ran Arsenal's football operations largely without the help of a sporting director. He was open to the idea of data helping to guide decisions, unlike many of his English peers at the time, and allegedly once signed Mathieu Flamini partly because he once ran 14 kilometres in a single match. Whether that was an ill-advised means of evaluating a player or not, the transfer at least offered an insight into Wenger's willingness to embrace numbers and new ideas.

Ivan Gazidis was CEO at the time, and he and Hendrik Almstadt, the club's head of business development, convinced Wenger to agree to the purchase of StatDNA by highlighting how poor deals for the likes of Marouane Chamakh wouldn't have happened if a data lens had been applied to the player's profile beforehand. Almstadt in particular placed the spotlight on two flaws attached to Chamakh's game to provide an example, with the first being that his expected goals numbers were low, despite his respectable scoring record for Bordeaux. His unsustainable finishing streak was coupled in with his lack of involvement in open play to provide a case against signing the French-born striker. Almstadt argued that Wenger would have benefited from such insight before chasing the player's signature in 2010.

Arsenal had previously paid around $250,000 to prevent StatDNA from working with other Premier League clubs, before later deciding to purchase the company outright. In fact, it wasn't too dissimilar to John Henry's attempt to absorb Decision Technology for Liverpool. Such is the covert nature of the data landscape in football that Arsenal tried to keep their purchase under wraps, with

Gazidis even referring to StatDNA as AOH-USA LLC in the club's annual general meeting. 'The company is an expert in the field of sports data performance analysis, which is a rapidly developing area and one that I, and others, believe will be critical to Arsenal's competitive position,' he said. 'The insights produced by the company are widely used across our football operations, in scouting and talent identification, in-game preparation, in post-match analysis and in gaining tactical insights.'

Stan Kroenke, who became majority shareholder of Arsenal in 2011, once described Wenger as one of Billy Beane's inspirations in an interview with the *Telegraph*. 'Billy Beane's idol is Arsène Wenger. You know why? His ability to spend money and extract value. That is what it is all about to be successful in professional sports. If you can do that better than other people, you are always going to be pretty good,' said Kroenke. StatDNA's vice-president of software and analytics up until 2021 was Sarah Rudd, a supporter of the club who also headed up Arsenal's data science division. A former software developer at Microsoft, Rudd had an educational background in business and computer science, and was also one of the first known people to blog about football analytics before exploring a role in the sport, similar to Graham. In fact, she landed a job at StatDNA after winning a research competition. A free data package was released by the firm as they searched for a new scientist, with Rudd's work proving to be the most impressive. Arsenal's decision to purchase StatDNA could have been revolutionary at the time, especially with Rudd holding the keys at the Emirates. The problem was that, despite acquiring the company and employing capable people, Arsenal refrained from truly empowering data and integrating numbers into their decision-making process like Liverpool did under FSG.

The Gunners began to drift under Wenger and struggled to challenge for the Premier League title as often as they once had. New people were appointed to modernise the club, such as Sven Mislintat who arrived from Borussia Dortmund in 2017 to oversee Arsenal's recruitment. The German, who had previously worked with Jürgen Klopp, lasted just 14 months. Wenger departed in the summer of 2018, and Gazidis, who had been CEO for around nine years, also left months later to join AC Milan. Raul Sanllehi and Vinai Venkatesham succeeded Gazidis in co-leadership roles before the former left in 2020. Arsenal weathered a storm of upheaval for years around Wenger's retirement. Their head of performance, Darren Burgess, left after two years, in 2019. Their replacement for Wenger, Unai Emery, was sacked before Christmas of 2019 after less than 18 months at the helm. Tony Colbert, a fitness coach, left after 20 years at the club. Neil Banfield, a first-team coach, left after 21 years. Gerry Payton, a goalkeeping coach, left after 15 years. All in all, Arsenal moved away from the necessary degree of stability to begin using data-charged insights to truly guide their strategy and thought process, and when they did have that necessary constancy, old habits prevailed.

When Edu, a former player under Wenger, was appointed as technical director in 2019, he moved to refine Arsenal's scouting department and talked openly about his intentions to incorporate StatDNA into his decision-making process. 'I want to work with fewer people. I want to work a lot more with StatDNA, which we have internally here at the club. It is very important,' he said. Several members of the club's scouting network who covered France, Spain, Scotland, Italy, Germany and Belgium were made redundant as Edu attempted to streamline Arsenal's operation, moving data-driven thinkers such as Ben Knapper, who became Norwich City's new sporting director in 2023, and Mark Curtis into recruitment roles from performance analysis backgrounds. However, just as he started to shape his desired structure, Rudd left to help establish Blue Crow Analytics, a new sports technology company, before founding SRC, a football consultancy, with her husband and fellow analytics pioneer Ravi Ramineni.

Everywhere you look, there are examples of clubs overlooking their analysts and sophisticated departments because of staff turnover behind the scenes, or because prominent executives prefer to make expensive decisions based on gut feelings, politics or recommendations made by agents. Barcelona perhaps offer the best illustration. Between 2014 and 2020, Josep Maria Bartomeu was president of the Catalan giants, having been elected by members of the club. The Spaniard oversaw the decline of Barcelona, dedicating extortionate transfer fees and excessive wages to Philippe Coutinho, Ousmane Dembélé and Antoine Griezmann in particular. While giving a talk at Turing Fest in 2022, Graham touched on the departure of Coutinho from Anfield, stating the Brazilian's underlying statistics during his time at Barcelona were around average for his career – largely based on his time at Liverpool – yet the Spanish club still seemed disappointed with what they had purchased. Two seasons later he was loaned to Bayern Munich, with Graham left questioning whether Barcelona had truly demonstrated efficient recruitment. Four and a half years after he was signed from Liverpool for well over £100m, Coutinho was sold to Aston Villa for around £18m, before joining Qatari club Al-Duhail on loan just one year later.

Barcelona spent roughly £230m in transfer fees on Arda Turan, André Gomes, Paco Alcácer, Malcom, Clément Lenglet, Nélson Semedo and Paulinho during Bartomeu's reign, with Lionel Messi in tears as he was forced to leave the club in 2021 after they couldn't afford to keep him. They essentially offered a clinic on how not to recruit players. Since winning the Champions League in 2015, the Catalan club has progressed beyond the quarter-final stage of the illustrious European competition on just one occasion, failing to escape the group stage in 2021/22 for the first time in over 20 years, and then doing the same the following season. The modern Barcelona were a mess in the public eye, selling future TV revenues in 2022 to fund transfer moves for big-name players, but beneath the surface things were totally different. Despite the club's relative turmoil, Barcelona had one of the most cultured analytics departments in world football, but it was simply being ignored by the people in power. They established their Innovation Hub in 2017, a department that acts as a laboratory of sorts for research projects and new ideas, teaming up with universities, offering development programmes to aspiring analysts and staging regular conferences featuring experts from around the world.

Graham appeared at the Barça Sports Technology Symposium in 2019, with one of his more interesting remarks being that a two per cent improvement in performance from one season to the next has a 45 per cent chance of delivering fewer points. 'Data analysis requires buy-in and time' read a headline on one of his slides, which, in a strange sort of way, could have almost been interpreted as a cheap shot at the club hosting the event. Unlike common practice in football, Barcelona have demonstrated a willingness to share knowledge and insights through their Innovation Hub – covering topics such as medical services, social sciences, performance and team sports – with the goal of building a community around ideas while creating an internationally renowned research and development centre.

Javier Fernández was one of the top minds to emerge from Barcelona, having been promoted from lead data scientist to head of sports analytics in 2018. With a background in software development and AI, he worked with coaches at Barcelona to translate tactical concepts into algorithms and statistical models. Fernández and his colleagues produced similar work to Will Spearman, using tracking data to interpret space and generate interactive pitch visualisations. Just like Liverpool, Barcelona had the tracking data and the technical expertise to create their own pitch control models, valuing different spaces on the pitch and adding context to match situations. In 2021, Fernández left his role at the Camp Nou to become a senior data scientist at Zelus Analytics, another newly established sports analytics company, like Blue Crow Analytics and SRC, hoping to provide intelligence as an external service for professional clubs. Even without Fernández, Barcelona still have an elite department on their hands, but it seems destined to be neglected by the club's executives on the football side of the business.

Working with data can be a thankless task in football, which explains why start-ups such as Zelus, Blue Crow and SRC are becoming increasingly popular. Speaking to *The Independent*, David Sumpter, author of *Soccermatics*, said, 'A lot of teams have people who crunch the numbers, but they aren't actually maximising the talents of those people or willing to do so.' One of Zelus's co-founders was Luke Bornn, former head of analytics at AS Roma when Mohamed Salah and Alisson Becker made their respective transfer moves to the Italian capital. 'These were players that had historically been undervalued at other teams. We saw that their value was higher than the market suggested,' he said. The former professor of statistics at Harvard University and pioneer of data science across multiple different sports has first-hand experience of the inner workings of numerous clubs. 'The thing that caught me off guard the most was how interested teams were in data, but then how little the data actually influenced decision-making,' he said. 'You'll have an ownership group who wants to invest in data. They might bring in an analyst and pay for some data but in the end, the impact of that role is almost nil.'

Bornn shares many of the same thoughts as Graham regarding football, with the pair aligned in their belief that recruitment is almost everything. 'My role was thinking about making objective decisions up and down the organisation, starting at recruitment and working through to sports science and tactics and so on,' said Bornn of his time in Rome. 'I tend to believe that, across sports, the number one lever that teams have to create wins is recruitment; putting the best players on the pitch.' The Canadian also shared similar thoughts to Graham on the concept of using goal difference as a currency. 'The unit of measure in each sport is different. In baseball, it's runs. In basketball, it's points. In football, it's ultimately goal differential and understanding a player's impact on goal differential. I have a very strong suspicion that if you asked a very experienced scout, "What is this player's impact on goal differential?" You'd probably get a blank stare.'

Bornn formed RedBall Acquisition Corp in 2020, alongside Billy Beane and RedBird Capital. RedBird Capital also purchased an 11 per cent stake in FSG in 2021 – investing $750m into the owners of Liverpool and the Boston Red Sox – and acquired a majority stake in Toulouse in 2020, appointing none other than Damien Comolli as president. Data-fuelled consortiums are becoming increasingly popular in football. ALK Capital purchased a controlling stake in Burnley in 2020, with intentions to build a multi-club network and overhaul recruitment using new technology and AI, having also invested in AiScout and Player Lens, two London-based football technology companies. Pacific Media Group also established a data-led multi-club model, acquiring stakes in Barnsley, AS Nancy, FC Thun, K.V. Oostende, Esbjerg, FC Kaiserslautern and FC Den Bosch. The owner of Brentford in the Premier League is Matthew Benham, a physics graduate from the University of Oxford, who also owns FC Midtjylland of the Danish Superliga. He made his millions through his gambling consultancy firm, Smartodds. 'Matthew is the X-factor,' Erik Sviatchenko, a former defender at Midtjylland, told *The Guardian* in 2015. 'His money is hugely important. But his use of statistics and mathematics is the extra thing that gives us the advantage. It is like Moneyball.' Several members of the Brentford board hold roles at Smartodds – or have previously worked there – including Phil Giles, who's now director of football at the Gtech Community Stadium.

Benham isn't the only betting expert who has graced the Premier League as an owner, with Brighton & Hove Albion achieving promotion from the Championship in 2017 under Tony Bloom. A fan of the club, the Seagulls were competing in League One, England's third tier, when he made his purchase in 2009. A mathematics graduate at Manchester University, Bloom's version of Smartodds was Starlizard, a company who describe themselves as 'data specialists' by using cutting-edge analytics to forecast results before placing informed bets. Speaking after he received an honorary doctorate of science from the University of Brighton in 2018, Bloom opened up about his background in gambling. 'I realised that applying mathematics and complex algorithms to sport, alongside other subjective techniques, allowed me to assess the probability of sporting events more accurately than the markets,' he said. 'Naturally, this was a significant advantage when it came to betting on sport. We use some of these same principles at Brighton when it comes to player recruitment, to assess players and their potential.'

The comparisons between Bloom and Benham are no coincidence. The former was once the boss of the latter at

Premier Bet. The company was founded by Bloom in 2002, and the pair famously fell out at the time, with Benham eventually fired and taken to court for his misconduct. Whenever Brentford face Brighton, the two owners are reportedly desperate to win for reasons beyond football. Bloom is one of Britain's most established gamblers and, alongside Brighton, he also has a majority stake in Belgian club Union Saint-Gilloise, who competed against Liverpool in the group stages of the Europa League in 2023/24. Multi-club ownership is a growing trend and those who recognise the perks of possessing their own football network also tend to appreciate the powers of data.

Both Brentford and Brighton are scientific institutions, although Benham and Bloom were forced to grow their childhood clubs organically from the doldrums. The two started their respective journeys far away from the glitz and glamour of the Premier League, whereas Liverpool and FSG have profited from an established base immersed in historic triumphs, coupled with a limitless ceiling. The subtle edges acquired by Brentford and Brighton resulted in promotion and mid-table finishes. Those same edges, once applied by Liverpool, delivered world dominance and pretty much every trophy under the sun. Brentford and Brighton are the Oakland Athletics. Liverpool are the Boston Red Sox, having used similar ideas to other smart clubs on the continent but on a much greater scale, with more resources and far better players. 'It's Liverpool, Brentford and Brighton,' said Graham in 2023 when asked about the implementation of data at clubs in the Premier League.

City Football Group possesses perhaps the most recognised global network of clubs, having expanded their portfolio to 12 in 2022 through the acquisition of Italian club Palermo FC. Manchester City form the heart of their football kingdom, rivalling Liverpool at the pinnacle of the Premier League. In the early days of City's emergence as a force, the Etihad club attacked the transfer market with cash on the hip, throwing endless amounts of money at problems in order to solve them. They weren't perceived as particularly efficient or guided by numbers before Liverpool's evolution under Jürgen Klopp, which seemed to have an impact on their appreciation for what numbers can do.

Beane has referenced the ripple effects that often follow when unconventional practices begin to deliver success for heavyweight clubs:

> In Oakland, we could have operated within this little space and nobody would have cared, but when you have a bigger club like Liverpool or the Red Sox, when they start applying objective decision-making, that's what changes the game because it forces the big clubs from the top down. You'll start to see a domino approach because they have to adjust. Every year, Liverpool have spent less than the top six clubs. They've spent incredibly wisely and are incredibly efficient. Ultimately, the top clubs will have to adjust to the way they are doing things, otherwise the efficiency will continue to overwhelm everybody.

Much like the ripple effects of Manchester United's success in 1999 after using Prozone, it was natural for City to wonder how their biggest competitors were keeping up with them on the pitch despite the difference in wealth between the two clubs. The City equivalent to Graham was appointed in 2014 after the Manchester club launched their 'MCFC Analytics' initiative to source data scientists, with Lee Mooney occupying the role. He was promoted to head of data insights and decision technology in 2015, but was technically employed by City Football Group and tasked with supporting every club under their umbrella. Like many others in his field such as Rudd, Ramineni, Fernández, Bornn and the likes, Mooney soon departed from his role to establish his own start-up, and he was replaced internally by Brian Prestidge in early 2020. The Scot was tasked with reducing the gap between City and Liverpool in the science department. Prestidge restructured his wing and made a series of additions to his team. Ravi Mistry was appointed as football intelligence officer, John-Mark Sisman was appointed as performance physicist, Chris Baker, who holds a degree in physics and is a qualified science teacher, was appointed as talent ID coordinator, and perhaps most notably of all, Laurie Shaw joined as lead AI scientist.

Another astrophysicist who once blogged about football, the Cambridge University PhD holder possessed quite the background upon his appointment at the start of 2021. Shaw's past roles included head of statistics and model development for the Treasury, research scientist at Harvard University – where he was also a member of their Sports Analytics Lab – and quantitative researcher for Winton, a research-based investment management company. Similar to Liverpool's Spearman, Shaw had experience of unearthing findings from tracking data. Within the world of data science in football, his appointment could have been deemed as a statement signing of sorts. City wanted to become more efficient and more intelligent after spending an excessive amount to evolve at the beginning of Sheikh Mansour's reign as owner. Gavin Fleig expressed as much in an interview with *Forbes* in 2012. 'At Manchester City, there has been a lot of money to spend,' said the club's former head of performance analysis. 'Now, undervalued talent was the focus of *Moneyball* in baseball. Our focus in the last three years has not necessarily been finding undervalued talent, although that is an extremely important element of our future going forward given our business desire to operate within our means.'

Fleig is now the director of talent management across City Football Group and, since his interview, it's reasonable to suggest that City have stuck to their initial plan so far. Over a decade has passed since Fleig talked to *Forbes*, with the Etihad club now appearing capable of funding expensive transfer moves by selling internal prospects, unlike at the beginning of Mansour's tenure, such as Cole Palmer, James Trafford, Roméo Lavia, Carlos Forbs, Shea Charles and Gavin Bazunu. Fleig occupies a leading role, and the same applies to Prestidge, but both met at Bolton Wanderers in the noughties.

Sam Allardyce, despite his reputation as an old-school traditionalist, was quite the radical thinker when he first emerged on the managerial scene. For all the gains acquired by the likes of Liverpool, Tottenham Hotspur, Arsenal, Brentford, Brighton, Aston Villa and other Premier League clubs over the years, he was arguably the first manager to lean on data to really find a strategic edge. Bolton didn't necessarily have a data science department or a scientist equivalent to Graham employed within their ranks, but they did have an established analysis department. 'In my opinion, it was the most advanced department at that time, and certainly had the greatest impact on the team in the way in which Sam and his coaches embraced analysis,' said Fleig. 'They built it into their game model, and allowed it to contribute towards Allardyce's development of scouting and recruitment, working with sports science and medical departments in terms of tracking players' fitness levels and availability.' Dave Fallows, now a scout for Liverpool, was employed by Bolton at the time, and Mike Forde, who later became director of football at Chelsea, was performance director. Allardyce had quite the team behind the team at the Reebok Stadium, and Bolton even managed to qualify for the UEFA Cup in 2004/05. Liverpool's version of an in-house analysis department wasn't created until Michael Edwards joined the club, four years after Allardyce left his post at Bolton.

The constant search for edges isn't a new phenomenon, but as has always been the case, some clubs are more interested in innovation than others. Based on modern evidence, the wealthier and more established clubs tend to be lazier when making decisions. Those who think outside the box tend to originate from further down the food chain, because smartness is not a choice when resources are scarce, it's a necessity in order to survive and climb. Some of the innovations generated by Liverpool are unique, but a selection of other clubs from across Europe have produced comparable work. Departments dedicated to data science are becoming the norm. Graham's desire to assess players according to their individual impact on points and goal difference was at least partially achieved by Sam Green at Aston Villa, and likely several others. Spearman's progress with tracking data wasn't too dissimilar to that produced by Fernández during his spell at Barcelona.

Liverpool's advantage existed as a combination of everything. FSG worked quickly to foster a data-driven culture that was ahead of its time at Anfield. Liverpool's approach was defined by the people in the boardroom, and that leadership filtered down throughout the fabric of the organisation. The right people were appointed in the right roles. Experts were presented with freedom, and they were listened to. Insights were valued and used to inform decisions. And in addition to all of those details, Liverpool benefited from an obvious upper hand in comparison to most clubs due to their wealth and status in the world of football, with a unicorn coach like Klopp in charge of managing the players. Combining every one of those ingredients produced a true juggernaut.

Chapter Fourteen

The Rise of the Machines

SLOAN HOSTED a discussion in 2022, titled 'Beyond Expected Goals: Analysing and Implementing the Next Phase of Soccer Analytics'. Ted Knutson moderated the talk, and he introduced proceedings with a bang:

> For years, this panel asked, 'When would soccer see widespread use of data and analytics in the sport?' It is now March 2022, and that question has been conclusively answered. It is now. Hundreds of teams from around the world use data and analytics in this sport every day. They don't necessarily use it well and they don't always use the best data, but it is no longer the unknown frontier.

After decades of doubt, scepticism surrounding numbers in football has declined. Players, coaches, executives and, to a lesser extent, pundits appreciate the value of what data can offer. Knutson's company, StatsBomb, has a wide variety of customers stationed across different leagues around the world, from Borussia Dortmund to Wigan Athletic to Forest Green Rovers to LA Galaxy to Lech Poznań. Expected goals has been integrated into mainstream football coverage, mentioned on a regular basis on the likes of *Match of the Day* and *Monday Night Football*. Job adverts posted by clubs seeking data scientists are multiplying with every passing week. The boom has arrived. It's no longer an option for professional clubs to incorporate data into their decision-making processes, it's a must to prevent extinction.

Liverpool will hope their edge remains for the meantime, and they're miles ahead of some of their competitors in the field, but staying ahead, one could argue, is equally as important as getting ahead in the first place. It poses the question as to what lies in the future. How might football look in 10 or 20 years, and what's the next landmark for people in the data and analytics space to work towards?

Luke Bornn isn't surprised that teams are beginning to hire analysts and scientists by the dozen. 'The same thing happened in basketball ten years ago. The same thing happened in baseball 20 years ago,' he said. 'That's probably the main trend we'll see. Teams having someone in-house who can understand and interpret data, and ultimately – should they want to use that data – better understand tactics and player evaluation.' Football can learn a lot from baseball in particular. The changes that Liverpool and their rivals might undergo in the coming years have already happened in baseball. 'In the NBA, the average analytics team is four to five people. In baseball, it's probably eight to ten,' said Bornn.

Ian Graham constructed his own team of scientists at Anfield, but his work was limited by the manpower at his disposal. 'The level of technical sophistication required to extract information from tracking data, there's literally not a football club in the world that has the ability to do that to its full extent, not even the biggest analytics groups in football, like Liverpool or Arsenal. To fully dive into the raw tracking data and extract the full nuance of all these off-ball actions, no club is there,' said Bornn, who has a bigger team of scientists and engineers at Zelus Analytics – his sports data business – than the large majority of clubs in Europe.

Over the next decade, football can expect to witness an expansive hiring process in the data sphere, with some of those hires perhaps even made by a new breed of executive if baseball does indeed provide the blueprint for evolution. When John Henry first descended on Boston in 2002, the stereotypical general manager was a retired player who had withdrawn from the field in favour of the office. According to a study conducted by ESPN in 2020, there has been a notable drop in former players occupying an organisation's top baseball decision-making position since 2001, from 37 per cent to 20 per cent. Those figureheads have been largely replaced by Ivy League graduates, originating from any of the eight most prestigious schools in the US, such as Yale and Harvard universities. At the time of the analysis, the percentage of Ivy League graduates holding such positions had soared from just 3 per cent to 43 per cent. Theo Epstein, who was appointed by the Boston Red Sox after Billy Beane opted to remain at the Oakland Athletics, almost initiated the trend back in 2002. It is now the norm for PhD holders to be plucked straight from graduation and thrown into the world of baseball. Epstein no longer looks like an outsider, he's surrounded by like-minded people in power positions.

The influence of former players is still strong in football, and that perhaps explains why scientists and analysts tend to get overlooked. 'I often see that data scientists can be isolated at clubs,' Jens Melvang, a former footballer who's now working for Stats Perform, told Sky Sports in 2023. 'That's a shame because they are adding a lot of value. So the biggest obstacle is making sure these more technical people are part of the process.' Edu is Arsenal's technical director, David Weir holds the same title at Brighton & Hove Albion, and so does Darren Fletcher at Manchester United, although his role seems to consist of unconventional duties at times. Rio Ferdinand, former star centre-back at Old Trafford, believes in his own credentials to fulfil the role. 'Maybe one day if the right opportunity came,' he told *The Athletic*, 'I think I'd be f**king unbelievable at it.'

Evidence will rule ego in the near future, and people with scientific backgrounds could end up bridging the gap between the players on the pitch and the owners in the boardroom. 'You won't often see him in a suit. He isn't a go-getting, big-personality kind of guy. You'd probably think he should be standing behind the goal,' Harry Redknapp told *The Athletic* when speaking about Michael Edwards in 2020, who left his role as Liverpool's sporting director in the summer of 2022. Future occupants of the role seem more likely to assume the form of Edwards than Ferdinand, especially considering the growing demand for statistical literacy in the game.

Hybrid roles are growing in prominence in the sport, with modern coaches expected to have an understanding of the numbers and how to contextualise them. In early 2018, Piet Cremers joined Manchester City from NAC Breda to become a performance analyst at under-23 level. Over time he climbed the ladder at the Etihad Stadium and was later presented with a first-team role. In the position, he analysed performances using video and data before becoming an unorthodox coach of sorts, integrating as part of Pep Guardiola's coaching team while also working alongside data scientists and video analysts. He specifically spent time alongside Mikel Arteta, who's now in charge of Arsenal, with the performance analysts at the Manchester club dedicating much of their time towards individual players to improve them. Raheem Sterling was a particular example of interest, with work done behind the scenes to improve his offensive positioning and shot selection during his time at the club. Cremers later headed up City's analysis department, but decided to leave in 2022 to pursue his UEFA A licence at the age of just 27, with more and more professionals within the sport expected to contribute across multiple departments by combining different skills.

In 2021, Mark Leyland decided to depart Anfield after spending more than eight years on Merseyside. He was a performance analyst who was tasked with deconstructing Liverpool's displays after matches, but was poached by Newcastle United after Eddie Howe offered him a new-look dual role. On Tyneside, Leyland was asked to combine analytical work with responsibilities on the training ground with players on a daily basis. 'Mark has had a big impact, he's played a huge part in what we've done this season,' said

Howe as United secured a spot in the Champions League in 2022/23, ahead of Liverpool who finished fifth in the Premier League and consequently qualified for the Europa League. After just 14 months of representing the Magpies, City managed to acquire Leyland after the Englishman was presented with an international role as head of coaching and methodology across the whole of City Football Group. There are data scientists, performance analysts, coaches and those in between, but the lines that separate each role are fading.

The rise of hybrid data is another growing trend that truly escalated in 2021 and 2022, with providers such as Stats Perform and StatsBomb essentially generating their own versions of what Liverpool had established behind the scenes by combining tracking data with event data to evaluate performances. In 2022, Stats Perform launched Opta Vision, which combined Opta's own in-house event data – covering shots, interceptions, passes, tackles and the likes – with tracking data. Opta Vision was created as a single, merged dataset to deliver richer insights surrounding actions on the pitch, adding context almost like Will Spearman's pitch control work at Liverpool. 'By merging our tracking data with the best event data in football, we're able to deliver accurate and insightful metrics which give a more complete view of what's happening on the pitch,' said Melvang. The creation of Opta Vision opened up new metrics, such as line-breaking passes, expected threat and expected pass completion.

Their main competitors launched StatsBomb 360 to deliver comparable insights around 15 months earlier. Their goal was virtually identical: to add context around events on the pitch. Unlike Premier League clubs and Stats Perform, StatsBomb had to add context without having access to valuable tracking data, and they did so through the use of freeze frames. Instead of adding context by tracking the flowing movements of players for 90 minutes at a time, StatsBomb navigated the problem by attaching a snapshot of the whole pitch to every pass, every shot, every cross. The new advancement allowed users to know the exact location of every player on the pitch across thousands of in-match events. Similar to Opta Vision, StatsBomb 360 can inform users about line-breaking passes, passing lanes and defensive shapes by attaching a bird's-eye view from above to events. The two companies essentially reached the same destination by taking different routes. Liverpool, in keeping with their tag as trendsetters with their fingers on the pulse, were the very first customers to benefit from StatsBomb's new 360 product, signing a multi-year deal immediately upon its release.

Whenever a valuable tool emerges that could be capable of helping players or coaches in one form or another, Liverpool tend to be near the front of the queue. Ahead of the 2021/22 campaign, the club signed an initial four-year partnership with Zone 7, a California tech firm who use data to protect the health, potential and longevity of athletes by using a data-driven AI system. Jürgen Klopp's players had suffered from an insurmountable number of injuries during the season before, and the crisis almost prevented Liverpool from securing Champions League football. Virgil van Dijk, Joe Gomez, Joël Matip, Fabinho, Jordan Henderson and Roberto Firmino are just a few examples of players who spent extended periods on the treatment table, with Klopp forced to reshuffle his pack in order to cope. Liverpool had gradually established an impressive degree of control across numerous departments – specifically scouting, recruitment and tactics – yet injuries still had the power to ruin everything.

At the end of 2020, Liverpool appointed Andreas Schlumberger as head of recovery and performance, and also appointed Frigyes Vanden Auweele in 2022 as head of osteopathy, which is essentially a means of assessing, diagnosing, treating and preventing a wide range of health problems. After that bizarre 2020/21 season, Liverpool became obsessed with injuries. Zone 7 wanted to access the fitness records from that peculiar season before joining forces with the club. 'The first thing we do is analyse last year's data and give you a what if moment,' said founder Tal Brown in an interview with *iPaper*. 'A few days before this (injury) happened, this is what Zone 7 would have said.'

The platform began communicating results by way of an app to Liverpool's members of staff, with Klopp altering his training plans, team selections and individual recovery plans based on the new insights. 'Of course, it's impossible to predict which minute and which tackle will cause something. The Van Dijk injury, the Elliott injury, they're not predictable, but if a person is showing a certain pattern around how much they're running and sprinting that has been validated to be high risk, that's meaningful. You don't want to expose them to that pattern,' said Brown, who has described the Reds as 'pioneers in data science adoption'. Liverpool amassed fewer injuries than 13 of their Premier League rivals in their first full season in partnership with

Zone 7, reducing the number of lost days to injury by more than a third compared to the previous term, despite playing 63 matches in all competitions while competing for an unprecedented quadruple. 'Zone 7 has been a helpful resource over the last nine months, supporting our internal load monitoring systems to help optimise the level of care that the Fitness and Medical Team provides to each player on a daily basis,' said Conall Murtagh, one of Liverpool's fitness coaches.

The initial presence of Zone 7 seemed to have an immediate impact on player availability at Anfield but, in the season that followed, fresh problems emerged with a bunch of Klopp's players picking up issues that restricted them from taking to the pitch. AI doesn't yet have all the answers when it comes to injury prevention, and it could be a long wait before football experiences its eureka moment. Variance is guaranteed to plague the sport, but much like matters to do with recruitment and tactics, incorporating scientific practices can help with the challenge of keeping the element of chance at bay.

The use of machine learning and AI has been scarce in the field of football analytics, but it's emerging as a relatively new trend and could even begin to assist Klopp in the dugout during matches. Shortly after winning the Premier League title for the first time in 30 years, Liverpool collaborated with DeepMind to explore how AI could be used in football, with their findings published in a paper in 2021. Demis Hassabis is co-founder and CEO of DeepMind, and also happens to be a lifelong Liverpool supporter. The company employs scientists, engineers and machine learning experts to investigate the capabilities of AI across multiple different industries, and it was acquired by Google in 2014. Graham and his department joined forces with Hassabis and Karl Tuyls, who was one of the lead authors on the research paper and also went to university on Merseyside. Liverpool provided DeepMind with data on every one of their Premier League matches played between 2017 and 2019, with Tuyls suggesting that coaches could rely upon AI during matches in the future. He told *Wired*:

> We're trying to build assistive technology. We're not trying to build robots, we're trying to improve human football play. I don't think you will see big impacts in the next six months or a year, but in the next five years some of the tools will be more developed, and you could see something like an 'Automated Video Assistant Coach' that can help with pre- and post-match analysis, or can look at the first half of a game and give you advice on what could be changed in the second half.

Technology is advancing at such a rate that Klopp and his assistants could be considering insights from a robotic coach before too long. AI has the potential to spot patterns that coaches might not. When Player A does this, Player B does this, which opens up the possibility of tactical shapes being analysed for structural weaknesses in real time. If Liverpool can't find a means of breaking through an opposition defence, the solution in the future could originate from a computerised coach of sorts, with AI delivering the answer to the man in charge, who will no doubt take the credit.

Researchers involved with the paper also analysed 12,399 penalties collected by Opta from 2011 to 2017 – 436 of which originated from the Premier League – before categorising players into clusters according to their individual playing styles. The findings were used to forecast where certain players were most likely to hit a penalty, and whether they were likely to score, with the optimal approach deemed to be: kick to the side of your preferred foot. Liverpool reached three cup finals in 2022, two of which were decided in their favour by penalty shootouts. Data surrounding penalties is relatively limited, but the application of AI to determine where a player will shoot, even if they've never taken a recorded penalty, is certainly original, and it offers an insight into how football could look in the future.

Ahead of the 2022/23 campaign, the Premier League agreed a deal with Genius Sports, who acquired Second Spectrum in 2021, regarding the development of skeletal tracking data, also known as limb-tracking. The data consists of three-dimensional visual representations of players' skeletons. Rather than solely gathering singular location data on each player based on their centre of mass, tracking data now includes more points on the body, such as foot, knee, hip and arm locations to make up the players' animated skeleton. Think about Football Manager going from a two-dimensional to a three-dimensional match engine. The innovative technology is central to the semi-automated offside system that's beginning to make waves in football, having been trialled at the FIFA World Cup in

2022. The upgrade opens up the prospect of coaches and even medical experts analysing in-match situations from a different perspective, perhaps even from the viewpoint of a specific player on the pitch, as demonstrated by Jamie Carragher and Gary Neville on *Monday Night Football*.

Speaking at StatsBomb's football conference in 2021, Ajax's head of sports science, Vosse de Boode, explained how skeletal data could help goalkeepers in particular. As she watched André Onana make a save between the sticks, she noticed that his stance was wider than normal in comparison to the typical goalkeeper, but rather than correcting him, she instead decided to run tests using AI. De Boode found that Onana's stance was actually more efficient for him, as it allowed the Cameroonian to cover more space and react faster when making saves. In fact, his wide-stance reaction time was 20 per cent quicker, with Ajax consequently reconsidering their approach to coaching goalkeepers in certain situations.

Sky Sports ran a 'Future of Football' series in 2023, which involved contributions from different coaches from around the world giving their opinions on how the game might develop. Andoni Iraola, who's now head coach at Bournemouth, believes that data is a basic necessity in today's game. 'Right now, you cannot live without data,' he said. 'It is evolving a lot. It is much more precise than some years ago. Normally, I start with this. I say, before I start watching the games of my next opponent, "Let's go to the data, so we know what we are looking at." It is something that has a lot of importance.' Paul Hall, a first-team coach at Queens Park Rangers, put forward his belief that AI will eventually referee matches, with Joao Nuno

Fonseca, who has worked as a coach at Manchester City and Benfica, suggesting that holograms will soon have an impact on training behind the scenes. 'If you had the opportunity instead of static mannequins on the football pitch, imagine that they are moving,' he said. 'I predict in the next 10 or 20 years, because the technology is making a massive evolution, holograms on the training pitch will be something common in the future.' The possibilities are endless regarding the influence that technology could have on football in the coming years, but AI seems to be the subject matter that could really change everything, and not necessarily in a good way. The plot of *I, Robot* was perhaps a little dramatic, but there are a whole host of risks and concerns attached to the rise of the machines, both inside and outside of football.

OpenAI's ChatGPT, which stands for Generative Pre-trained Transformer, is a chatbot that uses natural language processing to generate human-like dialogue, and it experienced its first birthday in 2023. It can answer complex questions and respond with different pieces of writing from snappy one-word answers to bullet points to full essays, calling upon sources from the internet to gather its data. Anybody can access ChatGPT and, since its emergence, it has proved to be both extremely smart and very dumb at the same time, grabbing the headlines in the process. Users have relied on the chatbot to write songs, emails, recipes and cover letters, with universities becoming prone to being hoodwinked by the technology as students explore new ways to save time, or essentially cheat. On the other hand, there's evidence of ChatGPT not being able to recognise the correct answer to its own riddle, in addition to believing that 1+0.9 equals 1.8. The chatbot can formulate extensive and convincing articles on conspiracy theories. 'This tool is going to be the most powerful tool for spreading misinformation that has ever been on the internet,' said Gordon Crovitz, co-CEO of NewsGuard, a company that tracks online misinformation.

The growth in popularity of ChatGPT has naturally had an impact on industries across the world. Publishers are beginning to use AI to write articles for their websites rather than employing members of staff to do the same at a slower pace, with translators, programmers and graphic designers perhaps under threat of becoming extinct in the future. But what about football? A chatbot could technically have the intelligence and sophistication to eventually inform recruitment decisions, although that milestone appears far in the distance for now. ChatGPT is inclined to hallucinate or exaggerate facts, and the language of sport is unlike the natural language text that's used to train models, with terms such as shots, tackles and passes forming an entirely separate text within the context of sport. The hope, rather than chatbots effectively replacing people, is that AI will create opportunities and take care of the repetitive and time-consuming jobs that no human wishes to undertake. The intention is for the technology to be assistive rather than overpowering, and if that balance can be found, human endeavour has the potential to be maximised in a world in which AI has supervision over the dull and laborious jobs.

Brad Griffiths, the senior vice-president of innovation at Stats Perform, has touched on the development of chatbots in football. 'The natural language aspect of asking questions and having data presented back to you is really exciting,' he said. 'The one thing we have to be very mindful of – certainly in the space where we are talking about sports data and recruitment – is the fact you can't make mistakes. You have to be getting data back that you know is reliable and is correct.'

Some football consultancies are already making moves to integrate such technologies into their products. Soccerment, for example, is a company that helps clubs implement data-driven decision-making processes, and it's working to refine what's essentially a virtual data analyst. The Italian-based firm has a data analytics platform that already allows users to search for like-for-like replacements by clustering all of a player's actions and using them to define their nature on the pitch. In a case study on Bukayo Saka, Soccerment's virtual scout recommended Barcelona's Raphinha as a capable successor for Arsenal to target based on his actions in comparison to the man who was being replaced. Saka was labelled as a 'one-to-one explorer' due to his tendency to engage in plenty of one-on-one battles with his opponents while also creating danger through carries and dribbles. Whether Raphinha is attainable or not is a question for the human to answer, but as far as a basic recommendation goes, Soccerment's platform could have done a lot worse, with the two players in question even sharing the same preference to use their left foot.

The evolution has only just started. Football is far behind other sports, but it's starting to catch up. Ten years ago, very few players were being recruited because of their underlying numbers. In today's game, some players are being signed solely because of what their numbers look like. How might things look after another decade? The information surrounding players and how they behave on the pitch could be groundbreaking by the time Trent Alexander-Arnold retires. Liverpool's future disciples of Klopp could rely on AI just as much as the German has relied on Pep Lijnders and Peter Krawietz, his two allies on the Anfield bench. The availability of players could be dramatically improved by new advances in technology and fitness. If baseball has provided football with any evidence of what follows, Liverpool's next sporting director could emanate directly from Oxford or Cambridge rather than within a club environment, although that does seem unlikely. The data science department at the club could soon employ twice as many people as Liverpool continue their efforts to solve the impossible problem that is football.

Chapter Fifteen

Liverpool 2.0

IN 2022, Michael Edwards decided to leave Liverpool after spending a decade of his career on Merseyside. FSG made attempts to retain his services, but the Reds' sporting director had already made up his mind. Regardless of his success in the role, Edwards had always planned to cap his time at Anfield to a maximum of ten years, stating as much in an open letter to supporters. 'Ten years, that's a pretty long time in anyone's working life,' he wrote. 'In football terms, it is an era in itself, particularly at a club like Liverpool where the expectations and standards are never anything other than as high as the supporters deserve. I am a big believer in change. I think it's good for the individual and, in a work setting, good for the employer too.'

While change can certainly deliver benefits in some circumstances, FSG hoped to avoid any upheaval by replacing Edwards with an internal successor. In the years leading up to his departure, Julian Ward shadowed him as Liverpool's assistant sporting director, occupying the role for around 18 months before the official changing of the guard in 2022. The transition was supposed to be seamless, but shortly after Edwards left the club, Graham resigned from his post as the club's director of research and began serving his own 12-month notice period. He had also spent the past decade of his career at Anfield, and he had effectively completed his mission by constructing Liverpool's data science department from scratch, building a team of scientists, improving the club's efficiency in the transfer market and playing his part to help deliver every trophy on offer, from the Premier League to the Champions League and everything in between. He believed that his time at the club had reached a 'natural end'.

Graham's impending departure was initially kept under wraps, until shock news emerged surrounding Ward in the middle of the campaign that followed his appointment. Less than six months after Edwards had left, the man who had been painted as his successor handed in his own resignation for reasons that remain largely unknown. Like Graham, Ward would proceed to serve his notice period for the remainder of the season, with FSG suddenly presented with a real problem to navigate. After years of making optimal decisions behind the scenes, Liverpool were about to lose many of the brains behind their operation, and it was all happening at once. Edwards had already gone, and Graham and Ward were set to follow him out of the exit door, with loans manager David Woodfine also following suit after around nine years at the club. All four of those figures had attended numerous football conferences as a united party of nerds alongside Will Spearman, Tim Waskett and Dafydd Steele, but the gang had been broadly dismantled inside 12 months.

Around the same period, news surfaced that placed doubt on the future of the club's ownership status, with FSG reported to be exploring the possibility of selling some form of stake in Liverpool. Mike Gordon, who had historically operated as the most hands-on member of the American consortium regarding matters to do with football, took a step back from the sport as a means of sourcing potential investors. Years of stability had allowed Liverpool to flourish on and off the pitch, but after climbing to the summit of the game and winning virtually every available piece of silverware, the whole structure looked like it was destined to collapse. Everything was up in the air and, to make matters even worse, the Reds were struggling to showcase the same degree of domination on the pitch, with Jürgen Klopp unable to harvest the same level of performance as in previous years from his tired group of seasoned midfielders. After serving the team's demanding engine room for a lifetime, the likes of Jordan Henderson, James Milner, Fabinho, Alex Oxlade-Chamberlain and Naby Keïta looked spent, no longer offering the necessary industry and control to present Liverpool with a platform to govern matches.

The brunt of the criticism for not upgrading the midfield department in the previous summer transfer window – which was Ward's first at the helm – was aimed in FSG's direction, but Klopp was equally culpable. His unwavering loyalty as a person has paid dividends throughout his managerial career, as he's still yet to experience the feeling of being sacked, and he's regarded as an icon at Mainz, Borussia Dortmund and Liverpool. In this case, though, Klopp proved to be too devoted to his two captains in particular, always finding a way to incorporate Henderson into his team, who was 32 years old and declining at the time, while presenting Milner with a one-year contract extension as his solution to missing out on the signature of AS Monaco's Aurélien Tchouaméni, who decided to move to Spain rather than England in Ward's first summer in the job, joining Real Madrid. He signed just two and a half players during his short tenure as Liverpool's sporting director, in Darwin Núñez, Fábio Carvalho and Arthur Melo, with the latter acquired on loan from Juventus as a caretaker addition who could act as temporary cover for Klopp's jaded midfielders. The Brazilian spent 12 months on Merseyside, but failed to play a single minute of Premier League football due to injuries that plagued his season. The story of what actually happened behind the scenes during that strange summer window in 2022 remains under wraps, but the decisions that were made certainly enhanced Edwards' reputation. He had been out of the door for little more than a few months, yet Liverpool had already nosedived.

With Graham and Ward almost abandoning the Reds at the same point in time, and FSG exploring outside investment, the scientific identity that had been fostered for the past decade at Anfield seemed under threat. Everybody was jumping ship and decisions surrounding the squad no longer seemed to be as studied as before, with Klopp presented with a greater degree of control in comparison to when he first arrived on English shores. Although he publicly denied as much, news started to inform supporters of a subtle change in dynamic at the club. Klopp was reported to be more 'hands-on' than ever before regarding matters to do with recruitment, with the Liverpool boss almost following in the footsteps of Alex Ferguson and Arsène Wenger after winning the lot and acquiring more and more power at his club, having even been awarded the Freedom of the City of Liverpool at one stage, which is the city's highest civic honour. His position was curious and quite rare by modern standards, as he had technically been employed for longer than the typical sporting director, which almost rendered the need for one as less important. Edwards, Ward and their peers tend to look after the medium- to long-term interests of their clubs, but Klopp was already doing that and he was going nowhere any time soon.

By his side, Pep Lijnders had steadily grown in prominence as his assistant. His ability as a coach seemed to be enough for Klopp to favour him over his last long-term assistant, Željko Buvač, who abruptly left Liverpool in 2018 – nobody really knows why – shortly before the Reds transformed into Champions League winners. Lijnders eventually reached a point where he was leading the majority of the training sessions at the club's AXA base, with Klopp again depicting shades of Ferguson by overseeing his work as a more withdrawn figure who saved his energy for the weekend, making the biggest decisions and operating as the face of the operation.

Indeed, around the time Lijnders effectively replaced Buvač, Liverpool showcased an entirely different level by adding layers to Klopp's famous counter-pressing game, specifically in possession. Mikel Arteta stated as much, and that was part of the reason why the Spaniard attempted to attract him to Arsenal as his number two in 2019, until his offer was politely declined. The Gunners boss expressed how there was a difference playing Liverpool before and after Lijnders. Klopp undeniably developed a greater appreciation for the ball after working with his new assistant. The full-throttle coach who had previously expressed his desire not to dominate 80 per cent of the possession share was suddenly sending out a different message in his interviews. 'We really kept them calm with our own possession,' he said after beating West Ham United in 2023. 'That's what you have to do; the best way to protect your own offensive style is with finishing, but as long as you cannot finish it off, then you should keep the ball.'

Working alongside Lijnders on a daily basis seemed to have an understated but notable effect on Klopp. His brand of football had always been associated with thriving amid chaos on the pitch, but his second-in-command encouraged control, often through the use of possession, adopting elements of Pep Guardiola's magic formula. By the time Edwards left the club, Lijnders was feeding scouting reports to Klopp. In his book, *Intensity*, he detailed his findings on Luis Díaz after watching him represent Porto against Estoril, touching on his anticipation to intercept, his proactive approach to defending, his runs in behind defences, his ability to create shots in the penalty box and his speed on the dribble, concluding his assessment with 'I have no doubt' and claiming that he was the best player on the pitch. 'He is a game-changer,' Klopp responded. In fact, as Liverpool constructed their new-look team after allowing the likes of Henderson, Milner, Fabinho, Oxlade-Chamberlain, Keïta and Firmino to leave in 2023,

Lijnders advocated many of the new arrivals, including Díaz, Núñez and Cody Gakpo. The Reds also explored the signature of Matheus Nunes before the Portuguese midfielder joined Wolves and then Manchester City one year later, with Lijnders known to be a fan of him. Ryan Gravenberch is another player who vaguely reinforces the theme, considering his Dutch heritage.

The narrative that surrounds Lijnders is a curious one. For some reason, a section of the conspiracy theorists blame him for Liverpool's monumental struggles on the pitch in the 2022/23 campaign, accusing the release of his book as a distraction and suggesting that he had given away secrets by sharing intimate details about the club's inner workings. Towards the end of that dismal season, it was Lijnders who essentially designed the tactical solution to Klopp's woes, suggesting that Trent Alexander-Arnold should become an inverted full-back whenever the Reds had possession under control. By drifting into the middle of the park at times, the Scouse defender provided Liverpool with more control in possession, while also strengthening the team's safety net in their attempts to guard against dangerous counter-attacks upon losing the ball. Manchester City and Arsenal had been experimenting with similar ideas using John Stones and Oleksandr Zinchenko at the time, with both competing for the title at the business end of the Premier League table. Lijnders revealed that Alexander-Arnold's change in role was his idea during an appearance on the *Training Ground Guru* podcast, stating that he convinced Klopp to give it a try by placing his salary on the line.

'The team became compact again with the ball,' he explained after his tweak delivered an upturn in results and performances. 'The team came together again and we were really balanced, we didn't suffer counter-attacks like we suffered them before. A little change can be enough for layers to feel free and comfortable again. The counter-press was working. Ibou [Konaté] didn't have to sprint 60 yards with each ball we lost. If you dominate midfield, you dominate the game.' Indeed, after adopting the suggestion put forward by Lijnders, Liverpool proceeded to go unbeaten for the remainder of the season, winning seven matches from a possible ten. The adjustment proved to be so successful that it remained in place for the start of the following campaign, which effectively meant that in addition to directing many of Liverpool's training sessions and having an influence on recruitment, Lijnders had virtually installed his own system at Anfield.

It's perhaps no surprise, then, that Klopp sacrificed his own pay rise in favour of giving one to his assistant and his coaching staff in 2022. The German extended his stay on Merseyside until 2026 by signing on the dotted line, but rather than boosting his own salary, he rewarded the people by his side. 'I have been lucky enough to meet many, many people in football during my time in the game and I don't think I have ever met anyone with the energy and enthusiasm he has for this game,' said Klopp when reflecting on Lijnders. 'He is probably the main reason for it, because he is a real energiser. You know him, this man is on fire and our connection is beyond football things.'

To bring in the likes of Gravenberch alongside Alexis Mac Allister, Dominik Szoboszlai and Wataru Endō in Liverpool's first summer window without Ward, Edwards or Graham on call, Klopp basically had to appoint his own temporary sporting director. A Bundesliga veteran by the name of Jörg Schmadtke occupied the spot on a short-term basis, even though he had technically retired earlier that year, having left Wolfsburg after four and a half years in charge. He was experienced, that was for sure, but he had never operated at a club as big as Liverpool, and he was very different to the typical FSG executive upon inspection of Edwards and Theo Epstein as the two poster boys. Schmadtke had navigated a relatively impressive career in his homeland, but his appointment took supporters by surprise. He wasn't part of the next generation like Edwards, or even Damien Comolli for that matter. Schmadtke was recommended by Klopp's agent, Marc Kosicke, and shortly after he arrived he labelled himself as a 'service provider' in an interview with *Welt am Sonttag*. 'I was aware of my position from the outset,' he said. 'In the specific case with Klopp as my superior, it's even easier for me. Klopp is the pacesetter in Liverpool. In principle, I am a service provider; the assistant who is responsible for the implementation of ideas and activities.'

He made the landscape seem straightforward but, before him, Edwards was at the very least on level ground with Klopp regarding his authority and his influence on mapping the future of Liverpool's squad in the transfer market. Intentionally or otherwise, subtle elements of the structure and the hierarchy had changed at Anfield. FSG had basically given the keys to Klopp and his coaches, and nobody could really blame them. After spending the past seven years at the club and dragging everybody with him to the summit of the mountain, he was an idol in Liverpool. The Reds had initially benefited from running away from Manchester United's outdated model for success but, in plain sight, things had come full circle with Klopp gradually establishing himself as the modern iteration of Ferguson, albeit one who was liked a bit more by the average Scouser.

Inside Liverpool's data division, Graham was internally replaced by a very capable successor in Spearman. After his notice was served and his departure was confirmed, he was approached by several clubs who wanted him to replicate his work, but he turned them all down. 'I felt like I'd done it,' he said. 'It would have been crazy to work for just one club again.' Instead, he proceeded to follow in the footsteps of many prominent figures within his field, including the likes of Sarah Rudd, Luke Bornn, Javier Fernández and Lee Mooney to name but a few, setting up his own sports consultancy firm. Ludonautics vows to help sporting organisations 'improve their decision-making capabilities' with data-driven advice provided for clients regarding player recruitment and performance analysis in particular. Graham founded the advisory business shortly after he became unemployed, and he launched it alongside his sidekick, Edwards. The two had operated as a duo for more than a decade, joining forces at Tottenham Hotspur and Liverpool before linking up once more to sell their expertise to more than one club at a time across multiple different leagues, especially considering the likes of Spain, Italy and Germany are far behind England in the race to become the smartest.

FSG did proceed to sell a stake in the Reds, but only a minority one to an American firm named Dynasty Equity. Despite their U-turn regarding a full sale, the stretch of time between 2022 and 2023 almost felt like the end of an era for Liverpool. Two captains with a combined 20 years of service at the club in Henderson and Milner both departed for new challenges in the same summer. Firmino, who was the fulcrum of Klopp's original 4-3-3, followed them out of the door, and he took the system with him in many ways, with Liverpool deciding to shift towards a new-look dynamic that consisted of an inverted full-back, technical midfielders, and a more traditional striker who was a true poacher at heart. Edwards and Ward left after playing key roles in making FSG's scientific vision become a reality in the shadows, and the boffin who became one of the few architects of football's data revolution passed the torch to the genius next to him.

When the original data-powered version of Liverpool peaked, the Reds reached three Champions League finals in five years, and also amassed more than 90 points on three separate occasions, which has only ever been done on 13 occasions in the Premier League era. In the season that Klopp won the Champions League, his team delivered 97 points in the Premier League and lost only one match, against the eventual winners, Manchester City. Football is packed full of fine margins and 'what if' scenarios, but if Liverpool had won that match against Pep Guardiola's men rather than losing it, they would have been crowned champions of England and Europe at the same time, while also becoming 'Centurions' with 100 points and 'Invincibles' by navigating an entire Premier League campaign without suffering a single defeat. That's how close the Reds came to unprecedented immortality.

LIVERPOOL 2.0

In February 2020, Liverpool beat West Ham United by three goals to two in the Premier League, picking up their 110th point from the last 114 on offer. The Reds had won 36 and drew two of their previous 38 matches, stretching from the end of 2018/19 through to the middle of 2019/20. No team in Premier League history had previously accumulated more than 102 points over any 38-match period. In 2021/22, Liverpool won the Carabao Cup and FA Cup, reached the final of the Champions League and finished one point behind City at the top of the Premier League table. Again, fine margins, but the Reds came within just two wins of securing all four trophies in that season, which has never been done before in England.

To a certain extent, all of sport – but especially football – is susceptible to being dictated by the element of chance. Potentially historic and groundbreaking outcomes are in the hands of fate, in the lap of the gods. But just like in Las Vegas around the blackjack tables, a conscious effort can be made to keep variance under wraps, and to get the odds ever so slightly in your favour. You make your own luck, and after beginning a journey to gain an edge that was destined to be fuelled by science and mathematics in 2010, Liverpool proceeded to win the lot, becoming the first heavyweight on the continent to persuade football that numbers might actually be useful after all.

Works Cited

Allen, Clive, and James Olley. *Up Front: My Autobiography.* deCoubertin Books, 2019.

Archer, Kenny. 'Colin Trainor: from bigging up Klopp to the little details of the GAA.' *Irish News*, 17 October 2020, https://www.irishnews.com/sport/gaafootball/2020/10/17/news/colin-trainor-from-bigging-up-klopp-to-the-little-details-of-the-gaa-2100110/ (Accessed 30 November 2023).

Ashton, Neil. 'Michael Edwards is the laptop guru who did a number on Brendan Rodgers.' *Daily Mail*, 6 October 2015, https://www.dailymail.co.uk/sport/football/article-3262490/Liverpool-s-head-technical-performance-Michael-Edwards-laptop-guru-did-number-Brendan-Rodgers.html (Accessed 30 November 2023).

Austin, Simon. 'Damien Comolli: why I employ a "truth teller" at Toulouse FC.' *Training Ground Guru*, 30 June 2022, https://trainingground.guru/articles/damien-comolli-why-i-employ-a-truth-teller-at-toulouse-fc (Accessed 1 December 2023).

Austin, Simon. 'Ian Graham: how Liverpool integrate data, analysis and coaching.' *Training Ground Guru*, 15 June 2020, https://trainingground.guru/articles/ian-graham-how-liverpool-integrate-data,-analysis-and-coaching (Accessed 1 December 2023).

WORKS CITED

Austin, Simon. 'Ian Graham: the "one currency" Liverpool use to judge players.' *Training Ground Guru*, 11 November 2019, https://trainingground.guru/articles/ian-graham-the-one-currency-liverpool-use-to-judge-players (Accessed 30 November 2023).

Austin, Simon. 'Man City Head of Data Insights leaves after six years.' *Training Ground Guru*, 10 November 2019, https://trainingground.guru/articles/man-city-head-of-data-insights-leaves-after-six-years (Accessed 1 December 2023).

Austin, Simon. 'Man City land big signing in quest to be the best in data science.' *Training Ground Guru*, 17 January 2021, https://trainingground.guru/articles/man-city-land-big-signing-in-quest-to-be-the-best-in-data-science (Accessed 1 December 2023).

Austin, Simon. 'Piet Cremers: young analyst who's now a key figure at Man City.' *Training Ground Guru*, 19 January 2022, https://trainingground.guru/articles/piet-cremers-young-analyst-whos-now-a-key-figure-at-man-city (Accessed 1 December 2023).

Austin, Simon. 'Prestidge promoted to top data science job at Man City.' *Training Ground Guru*, 2 January 2020, https://trainingground.guru/articles/prestidge-promoted-to-top-data-science-job-at-man-city (Accessed 1 December 2023).

Austin, Simon. 'Schmadtke: I am Klopp's "assistant" as Liverpool Sporting Director.' *Training Ground Guru*, 31 August 2023, https://trainingground.guru/articles/schmadtke-klopp-assistant-as-liverpool-sporting-director (Accessed 1 December 2023).

Austin, Simon. 'Second Spectrum set for Premier League debut.' *Training Ground Guru*, 9 August 2019, https://trainingground.guru/articles/second-spectrum-set-for-premier-league-debut (Accessed 30 November 2023).

Austin, Simon. 'Why Liverpool hired a French start-up to turn video into data.' *Training Ground Guru*, 21 August 2020, https://trainingground.guru/articles/why-liverpool-hired-french-start-up-to-turn-video-into-data (Accessed 30 November 2023).

Bandini, Nicky. 'Fikayo Tomori: "In Italy, the game is more like American football."' *The Guardian*, 26 March 2022, https://www.theguardian.com/football/2022/mar/26/fikayo-tomori-italy-milan-england-world-cup (Accessed 30 November 2023).

Barra, Allen, and Emily Buder. 'The many problems with "Moneyball."' *The Atlantic*, 27 September 2011, https://www.theatlantic.com/entertainment/archive/2011/09/the-many-problems-with-moneyball/245769/ (Accessed 30 November 2023).

Barrett, Tony. 'David Moores ends his silence.' *LFCHistory.net*, 2023, https://www.lfchistory.net/Articles/Article/3038 (Accessed 30 November 2023).

Bate, Adam. 'Trent Alexander-Arnold's vision coach Dr Daniel Laby on the Liverpool player's improvement | Football News.' *Sky Sports*, 2021, https://www.skysports.com/football/story-telling/11669/12388859/trent-alexander-arnolds-vision-coach-dr-daniel-laby-on-the-liverpool-players-improvement (Accessed 30 November 2023).

Bate, Adam, et al. 'Tactics of the future: marauding 'keepers, no formations and all-round players.' *Sky Sports*, 2 August 2023, https://www.skysports.com/football/story-telling/11095/12929273/the-inside-view-on-the-tactics-of-tomorrow (Accessed 1 December 2023).

Baumann, Michael. 'Everybody wants their own Theo Epstein.' *The Ringer*, 27 June 2016, https://www.theringer.com/2016/6/27/16037390/theo-epstein-market-inefficiency-cubs-red-sox-undeniables-ca36fd494ba1 (Accessed 30 November 2023).

Bechtold, Taylor. 'How the "idiots who believe" in the analytics movement have forever changed basketball | The Analyst.' *Opta Analyst*, 15 April 2021, https://theanalyst.com/eu/2021/04/how-advanced-analytics-have-changed-basketball/ (Accessed 30 November 2023).

WORKS CITED

Bell, Jack. 'Two American buyers purchase Liverpool club.' *The New York Times*, 7 February 2007, https://www.nytimes.com/2007/02/07/sports/soccer/07liverpool.html (Accessed 30 November 2023).

Benítez, Rafa. *Champions League Dreams*. Headline, 2013.

Bezants, Jack. 'Brendan Rodgers' best David Brent-like moments.' *Daily Mail*, 1 May 2022, https://www.dailymail.co.uk/sport/football/article-10736093/Brendan-Rodgers-best-David-Brent-like-moments.html (Accessed 1 December 2023).

Biermann, Christoph. *Football Hackers: The Science and Art of a Data Revolution*. Blink Publishing, 2019.

Biography. 'Babe Ruth – biography, baseball Hall of Famer, MLB Icon.' *Biography*, 3 April 2014, https://www.biography.com/athletes/babe-ruth (Accessed 30 November 2023).

Bleacher Report. 'Liverpool: interview with new owner John W. Henry of New England Sports Ventures.' *Bleacher Report*, 26 November 2010, https://bleacherreport.com/articles/527436-liverpool-interview-with-new-owner-john-w-henry-of-new-england-sports-ventures (Accessed 30 November 2023).

Blood Red. 'BILLY BEANE EXCLUSIVE | Moneyball man who inspired FSG, Michael Edwards & Liverpool transfers.' *YouTube*, 19 July 2020, https://www.youtube.com/watch?v=Z3OonrqqaZ8 (Accessed 1 December 2023).

Boswell, Zinny. 'Future of football: the AI-wielding "unicorns" and neuroscientists changing transfers and recruitment.' *Sky Sports*, 10 August 2023, https://www.skysports.com/amp/football/news/11095/12928151/future-of-football-the-ai-wielding-unicorns-and-neuroscientists-changing-transfers-and-recruitment (Accessed 1 December 2023).

Bray, Joe. 'Gundogan compares "father figure" Klopp and Man City boss Guardiola.' *Manchester Evening News*, 8 April 2022, https://www.manchestereveningnews.co.uk/sport/

football/football-news/guardiola-klopp-gundogan-city-liverpool-23631226 (Accessed 1 December 2023).

BR Football. 'Pep Guardiola's philosophy: inside the mind of Manchester City's coach.' *YouTube*, 19 September 2018, https://www.youtube.com/watch?v=gbD8_IEq3K8&t=85s (Accessed 1 December 2023).

Bristow, Thomas. 'Why Arsenal passed up on the chance to sign Virgil van Dijk.' *The Mirror*, 25 December 2018, https://www.mirror.co.uk/sport/football/news/arsenal-passed-up-chance-sign-13775948 (Accessed 30 November 2023).

Carroll, James. '"An incredible impact" – Klopp praises Reds' work with neuro11.' *Liverpool FC*, 1 March 2022, https://www.liverpoolfc.com/news/first-team/451767-an-incredible-impact-klopp-praises-reds-work-with-neuro11 (Accessed 30 November 2023).

Carroll, James. 'Pepijn Lijnders and Peter Krawietz pen new Liverpool contracts.' *Liverpool FC*, 28 April 2022, https://www.liverpoolfc.com/news/pepijn-lijnders-and-peter-krawietz-pen-new-liverpool-contracts (Accessed 1 December 2023).

Cassidy, John. 'Why buy Liverpool F.C.?' *The New Yorker*, 6 October 2010, https://www.newyorker.com/news/john-cassidy/why-buy-liverpool-f-c (Accessed 30 November 2023).

Cavilla, Tom. 'The real reason Rodgers had portrait of himself at home when managing Liverpool.' *Liverpool Echo*, 20 June 2023, https://www.liverpoolecho.co.uk/sport/football/football-news/real-reason-brendan-rodgers-portrait-27155637 (Accessed 1 December 2023).

CBS News. 'Sold! John Henry buys Marlins.' *CBS News*, 6 November 1998, https://www.cbsnews.com/news/sold-john-henry-buys-marlins/ (Accessed 30 November 2023).

Cipriano, Chris. 'How Boston broke the curse.' *Bleacher Report*, 17 June 2009, https://bleacherreport.com/articles/201349-how-boston-broke-the-curse (Accessed 30 November 2023).

Conan, Neal. 'The man behind the "Moneyball" sabermetrics.' *NPR*, 26 September 2011, https://www.npr.org/2011/09/26/140813409/the-man-behind-the-moneyball-sabermetrics?t=1631806022066 (Accessed 30 November 2023).

Conn, David. 'Liverpool and English football were a mystery to me, says John W. Henry.' *The Guardian*, 12 October 2011, https://www.theguardian.com/football/2011/oct/12/liverpool-john-henry-fenway (Accessed 30 November 2023).

Conn, David. 'Liverpool may have overpaid for players, suggests John W. Henry.' *The Guardian*, 13 October 2011, https://www.theguardian.com/football/2011/oct/13/liverpool-overpaid-john-w-henry (Accessed 30 November 2023).

Conn, David. 'Liverpool's owners battle boom and bust after Boston Red Sox stumble | David Conn.' *The Guardian*, 12 October 2011, https://www.theguardian.com/football/blog/2011/oct/12/liverpool-boston-red-sox-henry (Accessed 30 November 2023).

Corless, Liam. 'De Ligt responds to claim Man Utd rejected him due to weight fears.' *Manchester Evening News*, 22 July 2019, https://www.manchestereveningnews.co.uk/sport/football/football-news/manchester-united-news-de-ligt-16625609.amp (Accessed 30 November 2023).

Cox, Michael. *The Mixer: The Story of Premier League Tactics, from Route One to False Nines.* HarperCollins Publishers Limited, 2017.

Dator, James. 'The NBA is at a breaking point with three-point shooting.' *SB Nation*, 10 March 2021, https://www.sbnation.com/platform/amp/nba/2021/3/10/22323023/nba-three-point-shooting-breaking-point (Accessed 30 November 2023).

Denne, Rebecca. 'Sports vision expert explains vision in football.' *RedBull.com*, 4 June 2021, https://www.redbull.com/gb-en/sports-vision-expert-dr-daniel-laby-trents-vision-interview (Accessed 30 November 2023).

Donegan, Lawrence. 'John W. Henry: Soya bean trader who transformed a team of has-beens.' *The Guardian*, 6 October 2010, https://www.theguardian.com/sport/2010/oct/06/john-w-henry-boston-red-sox (Accessed 30 November 2023).

Douglas, Mark. 'The "secret weapon" that has cut Liverpool injuries by half and advises Klopp on team selection.' *iNews*, 26 July 2022, https://inews.co.uk/sport/football/liverpool-cut-injuries-secret-weapon-klopp-selection-1761181 (Accessed 1 December 2023).

Doyle, Ian. 'Michael Edwards explains decision to leave Liverpool in emotional open letter.' *Liverpool Echo*, 10 November 2021, https://www.liverpoolecho.co.uk/sport/football/football-news/michael-edwards-liverpool-open-letter-22127172 (Accessed 30 November 2023).

Draper, Rob. 'Swanselona! How Rodgers has turned the Swans into the talk of the Premier League.' *Daily Mail*, 12 November 2011, https://www.dailymail.co.uk/sport/football/article-2060748/How-Brendan-Rodgers-turned-Swansea-talk-Premier-League.html (Accessed 30 November 2023).

Duff, Alex, and Tariq Panja. *Football's Secret Trade: How the Player Transfer Market was Infiltrated*. Wiley, 2017.

Eccleshare, Charlie, and Mark Carey. 'Underappreciated or overrated – just how good has Hugo Lloris been at Tottenham?' *The Athletic*, 20 August 2021, https://theathletic.com/2780933/2021/08/21/underappreciated-or-overrated-just-how-good-has-hugo-lloris-been-at-tottenham/ (Accessed 1 December 2023).

The Economist. 'How data transformed the NBA.' *YouTube*, 4 December 2018, https://www.youtube.com/watch?v=oUvvfHkXyOA (Accessed 1 December 2023).

England Football Learning. 'Brendan Rodgers: my football philosophy.' *England Football Learning*, 17 December 2018, https://learn.englandfootball.com/articles/resources/2022/Brendan-Rodgers-my-football-philosophy (Accessed 30 November 2023).

WORKS CITED

ESPN UK. 'War of words continues! Steve Nicol calls Liverpool's throw-in coach comments NONSENSE! | ESPN FC.' *YouTube*, 5 May 2020, https://www.youtube.com/watch?v=aRWFwN0hpWs (Accessed 1 December 2023).

Eurosport. 'Meet John W. Henry.' *Eurosport*, 15 October 2010, https://www.eurosport.com/football/premier-league/2009-2010/meet-john-w-henry_sto2494866/story.shtml (Accessed 30 November 2023).

Evans, Casey. 'Man United had 804 options and Solskjaer failed to pick the right signing.' *Manchester Evening News*, 12 November 2021, https://www.manchestereveningnews.co.uk/sport/football/football-news/united-solskjaer-failing-wan-bissaka-22150792 (Accessed 30 November 2023).

Evans, Gregg. 'Unwritten: when Villa signed a string of present-day stars – and finished bottom.' *The Athletic*, 26 March 2020, https://theathletic.com/1697778/2020/03/27/aston-villa-tim-sherwood-recruitment/ (Accessed 30 November 2023).

Fels, Sam. 'Billy Beane changed baseball, but he could never conquer the game.' *Deadspin*, 13 October 2020, https://deadspin.com/billy-beane-changed-baseball-but-he-could-never-conque-1845360264 (Accessed 30 November 2023).

Figueroa, Pedro. 'This day in Marlins history: John Henry becomes the Marlins owner.' *Fish Stripes*, 17 January 2014, https://www.fishstripes.com/2014/1/17/5317310/marlins-history-john-henry-becomes-the-marlins-owner (Accessed 30 November 2023).

Finkelstein, Daniel. 'Is it right to tell manager time is up?' *The Times*, 31 December 2005, https://www.thetimes.co.uk/article/is-it-right-to-tell-manager-time-is-up-nljlz7skdmr (Accessed 1 December 2023).

Finkelstein, Daniel. 'The science of sacking managers.' *The Times*, 1 November 2008, https://www.thetimes.co.uk/article/the-science-of-sacking-managers-bkpfpptw0hx (Accessed 1 December 2023).

Finkelstein, Daniel. 'Thierry Henry is still best in Europe, according to new Castrol Rankings.' *The Times*, 7 November 2009, https://www.thetimes.co.uk/article/thierry-henry-is-still-best-in-europe-according-to-new-castrol-rankings-gsp6c7wf007 (Accessed 1 December 2023).

Forbes. 'John Henry.' *Forbes*, 16 June 2023, https://www.forbes.com/profile/john-henry/?sh=20f316fb1194 (Accessed 30 November 2023).

Friends of Tracking. 'Liverpool FC data scientist William Spearman's masterclass in pitch control.' *YouTube*, 15 April 2020, https://www.youtube.com/watch?v=X9PrwPyolyU (Accessed 1 December 2023).

Garro, Adrian. 'It's been 15 years since Scott Hatteberg and the A's walked off for their 20th consecutive win.' *MLB.com*, 4 September 2017, https://www.mlb.com/cut4/15-years-since-scott-hatteberg-s-homer-gave-the-a-s-20-consecutive-wins-c2523347 (Accessed 30 November 2023).

Garro, Adrian. 'No player better exemplified the Moneyball A's than Miguel Tejada, and he should be in the Hall of Fame.' *MLB.com*, 2 January 2019, https://www.mlb.com/cut4/miguel-tejada-s-hall-of-fame-case-c301558442 (Accessed 30 November 2023).

Gavin, Robert. 'Sox owner's success driven by numbers.' *Boston.com*, 19 April 2004, https://archive.boston.com/sports/baseball/redsox/articles/2004/04/19/sox_owners_success_driven_by_numbers/?page=3 (Accessed 30 November 2023).

George, Alice. 'When the Yankees got the larger-than-life Babe Ruth.' *Smithsonian Magazine*, 23 December 2019, https://www.smithsonianmag.com/smithsonian-institution/when-yankees-larger-than-life-babe-ruth-180973795/ (Accessed 30 November 2023).

Gerrard, Steven. *My Story*. Penguin Books Limited, 2015.

Golen, Jimmy. 'Red Sox hire statistics expert.' *The Edwardsville Intelligencer*, 14 November 2002, https://www.

theintelligencer.com/news/article/Red-Sox-Hire-Statistics-Expert-10490382.php (Accessed 30 November 2023).

Gorst, Paul. 'Ian Graham was responsible for Salah as Liverpool lose hidden transfer guru.' *Liverpool Echo*, 24 May 2019, https://www.liverpoolecho.co.uk/sport/football/football-news/ian-graham-salah-liverpool-transfer-16323870 (Accessed 30 November 2023).

Gorst, Paul. 'Liverpool chairman left in tears after striking worst deal in club history.' *Liverpool Echo*, 27 March 2023, https://www.liverpoolecho.co.uk/sport/football/football-news/liverpool-chairman-club-history-18195631 (Accessed 30 November 2023).

Graham, Ian. 'West Ham United.' *The Football Laboratory*, 5 November 2006, https://thefootballlaboratory.wordpress.com/2006/11/05/west-ham-united/ (Accessed 1 December 2023).

Graham, Ian, et al. 'Game plan: what AI can do for football, and what football can do for AI.' *Journal of Artificial Intelligence Research*, vol. 71, 2021, pp. 41–88. *Jair.org*, https://www.jair.org/index.php/jair/article/view/12505/26683

Grier, Kevin, and Tyler Cowen. 'The economics of Moneyball.' *Grantland*, 9 December 2011, https://grantland.com/features/the-economics-moneyball/ (Accessed 30 November 2023).

'Has one league ever dominated European football like La Liga? | The Knowledge.' *The Guardian*, 22 May 2018, https://www.theguardian.com/football/2018/may/22/has-one-league-ever-dominated-european-football-like-la-liga (Accessed 30 November 2023).

Haglund, David. 'More Moneyball, same problems.' *Slate Magazine*, 21 September 2011, https://slate.com/culture/2011/09/moneyball-movie-the-numbers-are-good-but-the-story-is-still-bunk.html (Accessed 30 November 2023).

Hay, Phil. 'How Prozone sparked a football analytics boom.' *The Athletic*, 17 November 2020, https://theathletic.com/2193722/2020/11/16/prozone-analytics-rammmylvaganam-analysis-premier-league (Accessed 30 November 2023).

Herbert, Ian. 'Klopp beware: the numbers don't always add up at Liverpool.' *The Independent*, 8 October 2015, https://www.independent.co.uk/sport/football/premier-league/jurgen-klopp-beware-the-numbers-don-t-always-add-up-at-liverpool-a6687076.html (Accessed 1 December 2023).

Herbert, Ian. 'Secret to Beane's success: study of data that no one else had thought.' *The Independent*, 19 November 2010, https://www.independent.co.uk/sport/football/premier-league/secret-to-beane-s-success-study-of-data-that-no-one-else-had-thought-to-study-2137957.html (Accessed 30 November 2023).

Hughes, Charles. *The Winning Formula: Soccer Skills and Tactics.* Collins, 1990.

Hughes, Matt. 'Man City poach Newcastle's highly-rated coaching analyst Mark Leyland.' *Daily Mail*, 20 February 2023, https://www.dailymail.co.uk/sport/football/article-11771693/Man-City-poach-Newcastles-highly-rated-coaching-analyst-Mark-Heyland.html (Accessed 1 December 2023).

Ingle, Sean. 'How Midtjylland took the analytical route towards the Champions League.' *The Guardian*, 27 July 2015, https://www.theguardian.com/football/2015/jul/27/how-fc-midtjylland-analytical-route-champions-league-brentford-matthew-benham (Accessed 30 November 2023).

The Irish Times. 'Liverpool fans hope hedge fund wizard can work financial magic on Merseyside.' *The Irish Times*, 7 October 2010, https://www.irishtimes.com/sport/liverpool-fans-hope-hedge-fund-wizard-can-work-financial-magic-on-merseyside-1.660505 (Accessed 1 December 2023).

Jervis, Rick. 'New "Globe" owner has history in soybeans, sports.' *USA Today*, 3 August 2013, http://usatoday.com/story/money/business/2013/08/03/john-henry-boston-globe-profile/2615127/ (Accessed 30 November 2023).

JOE. 'Balotelli madness: Mario's top 20 moments.' *JOE.ie*, 2012, https://www.joe.ie/sport/balotelli-madness-marios-top-20-moments-41186 (Accessed 30 November 2023).

Jones, Neil. 'Firmino plays "12 different instruments" in Liverpool's orchestra – Klopp.' *Goal*, 24 November 2020, https://www.goal.com/en-gb/news/firmino-plays-12-different-instruments-in-liverpools/3anzon4xal1x56kec6qpdsc (Accessed 30 November 2023).

Jones, Neil. 'Modern day icon: Mohamed Salah.' *Goal*, 8 April 2019, https://www.goal.com/en-kw/news/modern-day-icon-mohamed-salah/1coltbvyttiny16d5au35kqq2d (Accessed 30 November 2023).

Katwala, Amit. 'Now DeepMind is using AI to transform football.' *Wired UK*, 7 May 2021, https://www.wired.co.uk/article/deepmind-football-liverpool-ai (Accessed 1 December 2023).

Klein, Christopher. '10 things you may not know about Babe Ruth | HISTORY.' *History*, 11 July 2014, https://www.history.com/news/10-things-you-may-not-know-about-babe-ruth (Accessed 30 November 2023).

Knight, Chris. 'Liverpool's former transfer chief on Carroll's deadline day move.' *Chronicle Live*, 27 February 2020, https://www.chroniclelive.co.uk/sport/football/football-news/liverpool-newcastle-andy-carroll-comolli-17828676 (Accessed 30 November 2023).

Knutson, Ted. 'The death of traditional scouting.' *StatsBomb*, 9 May 2016, https://statsbomb.com/articles/soccer/the-death-of-traditional-scouting/ (Accessed 30 November 2023).

Knutson, Ted. 'StatsBomb mailbag – who should Arsenal buy in midfield + more transfer shopping.' *StatsBomb*, 1

April 2016, https://statsbomb.com/articles/soccer/statsbomb-mailbag-who-should-arsenal-buy-in-midfield-more-transfer-shopping/ (Accessed 30 November 2023).

Knutson, Ted. 'Things we think we know about football – July 2013.' *StatsBomb*, 6 July 2013, https://statsbomb.com/articles/soccer/things-we-think-we-know-about-football-july-2013/ (Accessed 30 November 2023).

Kuper, Simon. 'A football revolution.' *Financial Times*, 17 June 2011, https://www.ft.com/content/9471db52-97bb-11e0-9c37-00144feab49a#axzz3JpkxLHBk (Accessed 30 November 2023).

Kuper, Simon. 'How FC Barcelona are preparing for the future of football.' *Financial Times*, 28 February 2019, https://www.ft.com/content/908752aa-3a1b-11e9-b72b-2c7f526ca5d0 (Accessed 1 December 2023).

Lake, Jefferson. 'Liverpool's takeover by FSG: inside the deal 10 years on.' *Sky Sports*, 15 October 2020, https://www.skysports.com/football/news/11669/12104163/liverpools-takeover-by-fsg-inside-the-deal-10-years-on (Accessed 30 November 2023).

Leavy, Jane. 'Why on earth did Boston sell Babe Ruth to the Yankees?' *The New York Times*, 30 December 2019, https://www.nytimes.com/2019/12/30/opinion/babe-ruth-yankees-baseball.html (Accessed 30 November 2023).

Lee, Joon. 'Inside the rise of MLB's Ivy League culture: stunning numbers and a question of what's next.' *ESPN*, 30 June 2020, https://www.espn.co.uk/mlb/story/_/id/29369890/inside-rise-mlb-ivy-league-culture-stunning-numbers-question-next (Accessed 1 December 2023).

Lijnders, Pep. *Intensity: Inside Liverpool FC*. Reach plc, 2022.

Liverpool FC. 'Klopp, Lijnders & Krawietz – managing success | presented by AXA.' *YouTube*, 7 July 2020, https://www.youtube.com/watch?v=hBATY17DdIo (Accessed 1 December 2023).

Liverpool FC. 'Liverpool FC – honours.' *Liverpool FC*, 2023, https://www.liverpoolfc.com/history/honours (Accessed 30 November 2023).

Liverpool FC. '"MAGIC" | Roberto Firmino described by his Liverpool FC team-mates.' *YouTube*, 2 June 2023, https://www.youtube.com/watch?v=hZznUN_u4-o (Accessed 1 December 2023).

Liverpool FC. 'Reds appoint Michael Edwards as sporting director.' *Liverpool FC*, 4 November 2016, https://www.liverpoolfc.com/news/first-team/241881-reds-appoint-michael-edwards-as-sporting-director (Accessed 30 November 2023).

Lowe, Sid. 'Xabi Alonso: "Spain benefited from players going to England."' *The Guardian*, 11 November 2011, https://www.theguardian.com/football/2011/nov/11/xabi-alonso-spain-england-interview (Accessed 1 December 2023).

Lusby, Jack. 'Jurgen Klopp employing modern techniques to improve players' "reaction speed" at Liverpool.' *This Is Anfield*, 31 May 2016, https://www.thisisanfield.com/2016/05/jurgen-klopp-employing-modern-techniques-improve-players-reaction-speed-liverpool/ (Accessed 30 November 2023).

Maddock, David. 'The big Red book: Rodgers reveals 180-page dossier on how to bring the glory days back to Anfield.' *The Mirror*, 27 July 2012, https://www.mirror.co.uk/sport/football/news/liverpool-brendan-rodgers-reveals-180-page-1174680 (Accessed 30 November 2023).

Maddock, David. 'Brendan Rodgers rejected Liverpool three times before agreeing to become manager.' *The Mirror*, 1 June 2012, https://www.mirror.co.uk/sport/football/news/brendan-rodgers-rejected-liverpool-three-858909 (Accessed 30 November 2023).

Marshall, Tyrone. 'The forgotten man of Manchester United's finest hour.' *Manchester Evening News*, 31 January 2021, https://www.manchestereveningnews.co.uk/sport/football/man-utd-treble-solskjaer-prozone-19702839.amp (Accessed 30 November 2023).

Martinez, Guillermo. History of performance analysis: the controversial pioneer Charles Reep.' *Sport Performance Analysis*, 27 November 2019, https://www.sportperformanceanalysis.com/article/history-of-performance-analysis-the-controversial-pioneer-charles-reep (Accessed 30 November 2023).

McCaffrey, Jen, and Chad Jennings. 'From outsiders to architects of the Red Sox golden age: 20 years in, John Henry's ownership leaves lasting legacy.' *The Athletic*, 6 April 2022, https://theathletic.com/3190555/2022/04/06/from-outsiders-to-architects-of-the-red-sox-golden-age-20-years-in-john-henrys-ownership-leaves-lasting-legacy (Accessed 30 November 2023).

McGrath, Ben. 'Bill James, the professor of Baseball.' *The New Yorker*, 14 July 2003, https://www.newyorker.com/magazine/2003/07/14/the-professor-of-baseball (Accessed 30 November 2023).

McNulty, Phil. 'Brendan Rodgers: why Liverpool sacked their manager.' *BBC*, 4 October 2015, https://www.bbc.co.uk/sport/football/34440168 (Accessed 30 November 2023).

McTear, Euan. 'Liverpool FC CEO Peter Moore on the balancing act of modernising the club while respecting its tradition.' *World Football Summit*, 10 October 2019, https://worldfootballsummit.com/liverpool-fc-ceo-peter-moore-on-the-balancing-act-of-modernising-the-club-while-respecting-its-tradition-2/ (Accessed 30 November 2023).

Meagher, Gerard. 'Eddie Jones credits Liverpool's role in Jonny May's wonder try for England.' *The Guardian*, 22 November 2020, https://www.theguardian.com/sport/2020/nov/22/eddie-jones-credits-liverpools-role-in-jonny-mays-wonder-try-for-england (Accessed 1 December 2023).

Miller, Max. 'Genius Sports brings skeletal tracking to the Premier League.' *BroadcastNow*, 27 October 2022, https://www.broadcastnow.co.uk/tech-innovation/genius-sports-brings-skeletal-tracking-to-the-premier-league/5175903. article (Accessed 1 December 2023).

'Liverpool FC: fans go wild as club gets new owner John W. Henry after days of turmoil.' *The Mirror*, 15 October 2010, https://www.mirror.co.uk/news/uk-news/liverpool-fc-fans-go-wild-254465 (Accessed 30 November 2023).

Moneyweek. 'Can John W. Henry really save Liverpool FC?' *Moneyweek*, 22 October 2010, https://moneyweek.com/30877/profile-of-john-w-henry-of-liverpool-fc-50946 (Accessed 30 November 2023).

Morgan, Will. 'A cross to bear: Liverpool's crossing addiction in 2011/12.' *2+2=11*, 20 July 2012, https://2plus2equals11.com/2012/07/20/a-cross-to-bear-liverpools-crossing-addiction-in-201112/ (Accessed 30 November 2023).

Myers, Alan. 'Former Liverpool owner Tom Hicks talks to Sky Sports News about his time at Anfield.' *Sky Sports*, 3 December 2019, https://www.skysports.com/football/news/11669/11876502/former-liverpool-owner-tom-hicks-talks-to-sky-sports-news-about-his-time-at-anfield (Accessed 30 November 2023).

Naylor, Andy, and Jay Harris. '"A Cold War": the rivalry between Brighton's Tony Bloom and Matthew Benham at Brentford.' *The Athletic*, 30 March 2023, https://theathletic.com/3029279/2023/03/30/cold-war-brighton-tony-bloom-matthew-benham-brentford (Accessed 30 November 2023).

NBC Sports. 'Beane: "I never regretted" spurning Red Sox, staying with A's.' 8 April 2017, https://www.nbcsportsbayarea.com/mlb/beane-i-never-regretted-spurning-red-sox-staying-with-as/1274323/ (Accessed 30 November 2023).

Neyer, Rob. 'Sabermetrics.' *Britannica*, 8 August 2023, https://www.britannica.com/sports/sabermetrics#ref1182350 (Accessed 30 November 2023).

O'Hanlon, Ryan. 'Crossing in the Premier League is a dying art.' *ESPN*, 25 October 2022, https://www.espn.com/sports/

insider/soccer/insider/story/_/id/34873092/crossing-premier-league-dying-art (Accessed 1 December 2023).

O'Hanlon, Ryan. 'Data nerd Ian Graham helped fix Liverpool. Now he wants to fix European soccer. Can he?' *ESPN*, 10 November 2023, https://www.espn.com/soccer/insider/insider/story/_/id/38857256/data-analyst-ian-graham-fixed-liverpool-wants-fix-european-soccer (Accessed 1 December 2023).

Osmanbasic, Adin. 'Pressing, counterpressing, and counterattacking.' *Spielverlagerung*, 5 March 2017, https://spielverlagerung.com/2017/03/05/pressing-counterpressing-and-counterattacking/ (Accessed 30 November 2023).

Paine, Neil. 'If Billy Beane is done with baseball, he's left an indelible mark.' *FiveThirtyEight*, 15 October 2020, https://fivethirtyeight.com/features/if-billy-beane-is-done-with-baseball-hes-left-an-indelible-mark/amp/ (Accessed 30 November 2023).

Palmer, Myles. *The Professor: Arsène Wenger*. Penguin Random House, 2008.

Parker, Garrett. 'John W. Henry: 10 things you didn't know.' *Money Inc*, 8 April 2020, https://moneyinc.com/10-things-didnt-know-john-w-henry/ (Accessed 30 November 2023).

Pearce, James. 'How Red Star helped spark Liverpool's era of European dominance.' *Liverpool Echo*, 22 October 2018, https://www.liverpoolecho.co.uk/sport/football/football-news/how-red-star-belgrade-helped-15310189 (Accessed 30 November 2023).

Pearce, James. 'Liverpool FC's transfer committee – who did what to bring new signings to Anfield.' *Liverpool Echo*, 2 July 2015, https://www.liverpoolecho.co.uk/sport/football/football-news/liverpool-fcs-transfer-committee-9575259 (Accessed 30 November 2023).

Pearce, James. 'Liverpool FC takeover: Joe Januszewski and the email which led to FSG's arrival.' *Liverpool Echo*,

16 October 2015, https://www.liverpoolecho.co.uk/sport/football/football-news/liverpool-fc-takeover-joe-januszewski-10277676 (Accessed 1 December 2023).

Pearce, James. 'Why Jurgen Klopp wrote "terrible" on Melwood board.' *Liverpool Echo*, 28 October 2015, https://www.liverpoolecho.co.uk/sport/football/football-news/jurgen-klopp-wrote-terrible-melwood-10343072 (Accessed 30 November 2023).

Pearce, James, and Simon Hughes. 'Inside Klopp's Liverpool – a season that flirted with immortality and ended in heartbreak.' *The Athletic*, 4 June 2022, https://theathletic.com/3326855/2022/06/04/klopp-liverpool-premier-league-champions-league (Accessed 30 November 2023).

Pitt-Brooke, Jack. 'How Liverpool and Tottenham became two of Europe's best-run clubs.' *The Independent*, 1 June 2019, https://www.independent.co.uk/sport/football/european/champions-league-final-2019-liverpool-fc-tottenham-hotspur-damien-comolli-interview-profile-a8932816.html (Accessed 30 November 2023).

Polden, Jake. 'Coutinho's secret Liverpool clause and five times Michael Edwards struck gold.' *The Mirror*, 19 March 2021, https://www.mirror.co.uk/sport/football/news/philippe-coutinhos-secret-liverpool-clause-23754319 (Accessed 30 November 2023).

Polden, Jake. 'Daniel Sturridge reveals Naby Keita's ball skills leave him stunned as he heaps praise on the new Liverpool signing.' *The Mirror*, 23 July 2018, https://www.mirror.co.uk/sport/football/news/daniel-sturridge-reveals-naby-keitas-12969501 (Accessed 1 December 2023).

Powell, Dave. 'FSG investors link up with former Liverpool sporting director explained.' *Liverpool Echo*, 26 January 2022, https://www.liverpoolecho.co.uk/sport/football/fsg-investors-link-up-former-22877722 (Accessed 30 November 2023).

Powell, Dave. 'Liverpool and FSG partners RedBird deliver on takeover promise at Toulouse.' *Liverpool Echo*, 26 April

2022, https://www.liverpoolecho.co.uk/sport/football/football-news/liverpool-fsg-redbird-toulouse-23784555 (Accessed 30 November 2023).

Powell, Dave. 'Michael Edwards secret weapon on what FSG told him about Liverpool transfer plan.' *Liverpool Echo*, 4 March 2022, https://www.liverpoolecho.co.uk/sport/football/football-news/liverpool-fsg-michael-edwards-23266824 (Accessed 30 November 2023).

Power, Paul, *et al*. 'Mythbusting set-pieces in soccer.' *Stats Perform*, 2018, https://www.statsperform.com/resource/exploiting-inefficiencies-at-set-pieces-sloan/ (Accessed 30 November 2023).

Pressman, Aaron. 'Red Sox owner, trader Henry sticks to plan.' *Reuters*, 3 May 2010, https://www.reuters.com/article/us-johnhenry-idUSTRE6425AQ20100503/ (Accessed 30 November 2023).

Raymond, Adam K. 'Theo Epstein doesn't just break curses, he builds dynasties.' *New York Magazine*, 3 November 2016, https://nymag.com/vindicated/2016/11/theo-epstein-doesnt-just-break-curses-he-builds-dynasties.html (Accessed 30 November 2023).

Razavi, Amir. 'Albion owner Tony Bloom says he bought club out of love, not for money.' *The Argus*, 3 August 2018, https://www.theargus.co.uk/sport/16397498.brighton-owner-tony-bloom-bought-club-love/ (Accessed 30 November 2023).

Reade, Brian. *An Epic Swindle: 44 Months with a Pair of Cowboys*. Quercus Publishing, 2011.

Reddy, Melissa. 'Barcelona have a data advantage – so why aren't they using it properly?' *The Independent*, 11 February 2022, https://www.independent.co.uk/sport/football/barcelona-transfers-data-analysis-signings-b2012240.html (Accessed 30 November 2023).

Ross, Casey, and Callum Borchers. 'John W. Henry, soft-spoken businessman with an appetite for risk.' *Boston.com*,

3 August 2013, https://www.boston.com/uncategorized/noprimarytagmatch/2013/08/03/john-w-henry-soft-spoken-businessman-with-an-appetite-for-risk/ (Accessed 30 November 2023).

The Royal Institution. 'Christmas Lectures 2019: How to Get Lucky – Hannah Fry.' *YouTube*, 3 February 2020, https://www.youtube.com/watch?v=_q4DrUHKC0Q&t=2124s (Accessed 1 December 2023).

Sansom, Dan. 'Romelu Lukaku: Thomas Tuchel says "not the time to laugh" about Chelsea striker after his seven touches against Crystal Palace.' *Sky Sports*, 22 February 2022, https://www.skysports.com/football/news/11668/12547978/romelu-lukaku-thomas-tuchel-says-not-time-to-laugh-after-chelsea-strikers-seven-touches-against-crystal-palace (Accessed 30 November 2023).

Schoenfeld, Bruce. 'How data (and some breathtaking soccer) brought Liverpool to the cusp of glory.' *The New York Times*, 22 May 2019, https://www.nytimes.com/2019/05/22/magazine/soccer-data-liverpool.html (Accessed 30 November 2023).

Shaw, Chris. 'In numbers: Bill Shankly's Liverpool reign.' *Liverpool FC*, 1 December 2019, https://www.liverpoolfc.com/news/features/374163-in-numbers-bill-shankly-s-liverpool-reign (Accessed 30 November 2023).

Shaw, Chris. 'Pep Lijnders on cup final, Kelleher, pathways and "team behind the team".' *Liverpool FC*, 25 February 2022, https://www.liverpoolfc.com/news/pep-lijnders-cup-final-kelleher-pathways-and-team-behind-team (Accessed 30 November 2023).

Shuttleworth, Peter. 'Swansea City's family man Brendan Rodgers' Wembley way.' *BBC*, 28 May 2011, https://www.bbc.co.uk/sport/football/13348276 (Accessed 30 November 2023).

Siregar, Cady. 'What is heavy metal football & how has Jurgen Klopp used it at Liverpool?' *Goal.com*, 15 November 2021, https://www.goal.com/en-gb/news/what-is-heavy-metal-football-how-has-jurgen-klopp-used-it-at/gvxzni0i7rne1enr3bayptwcr (Accessed 30 November 2023).

Sky Sports. 'Andy Carroll had to google Liverpool players – but returns to Newcastle "grown up."' *Sky Sports*, 20 August 2019, https://www.skysports.com/football/news/11678/11789227/andy-carroll-had-to-google-liverpool-players-but-returns-to-newcastle-grown-up (Accessed 30 November 2023).

Sky Sports. 'Jurgen Klopp wore Cristiano Ronaldo underpants before Champions League final, says Georginio Wijnaldum.' *Sky Sports*, 14 August 2019, https://www.skysports.com/football/news/11669/11785159/jurgen-klopp-wore-cristiano-ronaldo-underpants-before-champions-league-final-says-georginio-wijnaldum (Accessed 1 December 2023).

Sky Sports Premier League. 'Being an INVINCIBLE! | Freddie Ljungberg in-depth analysis with Jamie Carragher.' *YouTube*, 28 November 2023, https://www.youtube.com/watch?v=NA6XslCM-8E (Accessed 1 December 2023).

Sky Sports Premier League. 'Rafa Benítez & Jamie Carragher on how Liverpool won the Champions League in 2005.' *YouTube*, 10 December 2019, https://www.youtube.com/watch?v=zMKDSHl5PJg (Accessed 1 December 2023).

Sky Sports Retro. '"Work it out for yourself" – Graeme Souness' hilarious Liverpool stories.' *YouTube*, 14 July 2020, https://www.youtube.com/watch?v=fpwa-tgasYU (Accessed 1 December 2023).

Slater, Matt. 'From Barnsley to Belgium, the club owners taking on the elite with data, pressing and young players.' *The Athletic*, 3 April 2021, https://theathletic.com/2479880/2021/04/03/from-barnsley-to-belgium-the-club-owners-taking-on-the-elite-with-data-pressing-and-young-players (Accessed 30 November 2023).

Slaton, Zach. 'The analyst behind Manchester City's rapid rise (Part 1).' *Forbes*, 16 August 2012, https://www.forbes.com/sites/zachslaton/2012/08/16/the-analyst-behind-manchester-citys-player-investments-part-1/?sh=727942c3493e (Accessed 1 December 2023).

Slaton, Zach. 'The analyst behind Manchester City's rapid rise (Part 2).' *Forbes*, 16 August 2012, https://www.forbes.com/sites/zachslaton/2012/08/16/the-analyst-behind-manchester-citys-player-investments-part-2/?sh=c2dd616574a7 (Accessed 1 December 2023).

Smith, Rory. 'Can this man make soccer smarter?' *The New York Times*, 14 October 2023, https://www.nytimes.com/2023/10/14/world/europe/liverpool-ian-graham-data.html (Accessed 1 December 2023).

Smith, Rory. *Expected Goals: The Story of How Data Conquered Football and Changed the Game Forever.* HarperCollins Publishers Limited, 2023.

Smith, Rory. 'How Arsenal and Arsène Wenger Bought Into Analytics.' *The New York Times*, 3 February 2017, https://www.nytimes.com/2017/02/03/sports/soccer/arsenal-arsene-wenger-analytics.html (Accessed 30 November 2023).

Spearman, William, *et al.* 'Physics-based modeling of pass probabilities in soccer.' *ResearchGate*, 17 March 2017, https://www.researchgate.net/publication/315166647_Physics-Based_Modeling_of_Pass_Probabilities_in_Soccer (Accessed 1 December 2023).

StatsBomb. 'StatsBomb sign multi-year agreement with Liverpool FC.' *StatsBomb*, 24 March 2021, https://statsbomb.com/news/statsbomb-sign-multi-year-agreement-with-liverpool-fc/ (Accessed 1 December 2023).

Stats Perform. 'The art of crossing.' *Stats Perform*, 2017, https://www.statsperform.com/resource/the-art-of-crossing/ (Accessed 30 November 2023).

Stats Perform. 'Stats Perform to launch Opta Vision.' *Stats Perform*, 10 June 2022, https://www.statsperform.com/press/stats-perform-to-launch-opta-vision/ (Accessed 1 December 2023).

Steenbach, Kasper. '"I work on the long, fast and clever": meet Liverpool's throw-in coach.' *The Guardian*, 23 September 2020, https://www.theguardian.com/football/2020/sep/23/liverpool-throw-in-coach-thomas-gronnemark-klopp (Accessed 30 November 2023).

St John, Allen. 'Powered by Bill James and friends, the Red Sox win (another) Moneyball World Series.' *Forbes*, 31 October 2013, https://www.forbes.com/sites/allenstjohn/2013/10/31/powered-by-bill-james-and-friends-the-red-sox-win-another-moneyball-world-series/amp/ (Accessed 30 November 2023).

Stout, Glenn, and Thomas Dunne. 'The real reason the Red Sox sold Babe Ruth.' *New York Post*, 6 March 2016, https://nypost.com/2016/03/06/the-real-reason-the-red-sox-sold-babe-ruth/ (Accessed 30 November 2023).

Summersell, Chris. 'Are Liverpool breaking a sacred defensive code?' *Medium*, 25 March 2022, https://medium.com/@chris.summersell/are-liverpool-breaking-a-sacred-defensive-code-8c5f806a4c41 (Accessed 30 November 2023).

Sykes, Joe, and Neil Paine. 'How one man's bad math helped ruin decades of English soccer.' *FiveThirtyEight*, 27 October 2016, https://fivethirtyeight.com/features/how-one-mans-bad-math-helped-ruin-decades-of-english-soccer/ (Accessed 30 November 2023).

Taylor, Daniel. 'McClaren at the cutting edge.' *The Guardian*, 7 February 1999, https://amp.theguardian.com/football/1999/feb/07/newsstory.sport (Accessed 30 November 2023).

Taylor, Daniel, and Adam Crafton. 'Michael Edwards – the visionary behind Liverpool's remarkable rise.' *The Athletic*, 29 June 2020, https://theathletic.com/1896993/2020/06/30/michael-edwards-liverpool-premier-league-jurgen-klopp-sporting-director/ (Accessed 30 November 2023).

Thompson, Mark. 'Analytics is older than you think: (re)introducing Charles Reep.' *Get Goalside*, 13 May 2021, https://

www.getgoalsideanalytics.com/36315087-analytics-is-older-than-you-think/ (Accessed 30 November 2023).

Thompson, Stuart A. 'Disinformation researchers raise alarms about AI chatbots.' *The New York Times*, 9 February 2023, https://www.nytimes.com/2023/02/08/technology/ai-chatbots-disinformation.html (Accessed 1 December 2023).

Tifo Football. 'What Is Moneyball?' *YouTube*, 29 November 2016, https://www.youtube.com/watch?v=J36ZfXBsGjs (Accessed 1 December 2023).

Training Ground Guru. 'Edu: StatDNA will come more to the fore as part of Arsenal revamp.' *Training Ground Guru*, 11 September 2020, https://trainingground.guru/articles/edu-statdna-will-come-more-to-the-fore-as-part-of-revamp (Accessed 30 November 2023).

Training Ground Guru. 'Jack Wilshere: loss of "proper Arsenal people" has hurt Gunners.' *Training Ground Guru*, 10 May 2021, https://trainingground.guru/articles/jack-wilshere-loss-of-proper-arsenal-people-has-hurt-gunners (Accessed 30 November 2023).

Training Ground Guru, and SkillCorner. 'Which is the most physically demanding league?' *Training Ground Guru*, 23 August 2020, https://trainingground.guru/articles/which-is-the-most-physically-demanding-league (Accessed 30 November 2023).

Trainor, Colin. 'Borussia Dortmund – what's gone wrong?' *StatsBomb*, 29 December 2014, https://statsbomb.com/articles/soccer/borussia-dortmund-whats-gone-wrong/ (Accessed 30 November 2023).

Tuyls, Karl, *et al*. 'Advancing sports analytics through AI research.' *Google DeepMind*, 21 May 2021, https://deepmind.google/discover/blog/advancing-sports-analytics-through-ai-research/ (Accessed 1 December 2023).

USA Today. '"Throw-in nerd" challenges perceptions at Liverpool.' *USA Today*, 5 September 2018, http://usatoday.

com/story/sports/soccer/2018/09/05/throw-in-nerd-challenges-perceptions-at-liverpool/37715799/ (Accessed 30 November 2023).

Van Luling, Todd. '8 things you learned from movies that are actually lies.' *Huffington Post*, 8 November 2014, https://www.huffingtonpost.co.uk/entry/8-lies-from-movies_n_5666578 (Accessed 30 November 2023).

Wakefield, Mark. 'Jurgen Klopp bolsters Liverpool backroom staff with new appointment.' *Liverpool Echo*, 14 July 2022, https://www.liverpoolecho.co.uk/sport/football/football-news/jurgen-klopp-new-liverpool-appointment-24491813 (Accessed 1 December 2023).

Wallace, Sam. 'Pep Lijnders influence proves it is not just Jurgen Klopp pulling strings at Liverpool.' *The Telegraph*, 4 January 2023, https://www.telegraph.co.uk/football/2023/01/04/how-pep-lijnders-influence-has-grown-liverpool-following-anfield/ (Accessed 1 December 2023).

Watts, Charles. 'Arsene Wenger describes his football philosophy in his own words.' *Football London*, 17 July 2018, https://www.football.london/arsenal-fc/news/latest-arsenal-news-arsene-wenger-14916999 (Accessed 1 December 2023).

Whitwell, Laurie. 'Premier League – Rio Ferdinand: player, pundit, influencer … sporting director? "I think I'd be f***ing unbelievable at it."' *The Athletic*, 5 November 2021, https://theathletic.com/2936593/2021/11/06/premier-league-rio-ferdinand-player-pundit-influencer-sporting-director/ (Accessed 1 December 2023).

Wigmore, Tim. 'Moreyball: how data "idiots" took over the Houston Rockets and revolutionised basketball.' *iNews*, 14 December 2017, https://inews.co.uk/sport/moreyball-houston-rockets-three-pointers-110791 (Accessed 30 November 2023).

Williams, Sam. 'Behind the badge: the physicist who leads Liverpool's data department.' *Liverpool FC*, 15 June

2020, https://www.liverpoolfc.com/news/behind-the-badge/398645-ian-graham-liverpool-fc-behind-the-badge (Accessed 30 November 2023).

Williams, Sam. 'The "weird" journey of William Spearman, LFC's lead data scientist.' *Liverpool FC*, 2 February 2022, https://www.liverpoolfc.com/news/first-team/450917-the-weird-journey-of-william-spearman-liverpool-s-lead-data-scientist (Accessed 30 November 2023).

Williams, Tom. 'Michael Edwards: the making of the man who helped to make Klopp's Liverpool.' *Bleacher Report*, 25 March 2020, https://bleacherreport.com/articles/2882599-michael-edwards-the-making-of-the-man-who-helped-to-make-klopps-liverpoool (Accessed 30 November 2023).

Williams-Grut, Oscar. 'The inside story on Britain's greatest sports gambler – and the company that helps him win.' *The Journal*, 14 February 2016, https://www.thejournal.ie/tony-bloom-starlizard-2597458-Feb2016/ (Accessed 30 November 2023).

Wilson, Jeremy. 'Arsenal owner Stan Kroenke: Arsène Wenger is one of the greats – he will be in charge for as long as he wants.' *The Telegraph*, 30 September 2011, https://www.telegraph.co.uk/sport/football/teams/arsenal/8797931/Arsenal-owner-Stan-Kroenke-Arsene-Wenger-is-one-of-the-greats-he-will-be-in-charge-for-as-long-as-he-wants.html (Accessed 30 November 2023).

Wilson, Jeremy. 'Revealed: the Silicon Valley algorithm helping Liverpool cope with history-making quadruple assault.' *The Telegraph*, 18 May 2022, https://www.telegraph.co.uk/football/2022/05/18/revealed-silicon-valley-algorithm-helping-liverpool-cope-history/ (Accessed 1 December 2023).

Wilson, Jonathan. 'The question: how important is possession?' *The Guardian*, 12 May 2010, https://www.theguardian.com/sport/blog/2010/may/12/the-question-important-possession (Accessed 30 November 2023).

Wright, Chris. 'Man City owners buy 11th club: how much success have they had around the world?' *ESPN*, 5 July 2022, https://www.espn.com/soccer/story/_/id/37629792/how-much-success-had-world (Accessed 30 November 2023).

'Zone7 expands service to Liverpool FC.' *Zone7*, 19 May 2022, https://zone7.ai/news/client-announcements/zone7-expands-service-to-liverpool-fc/ (Accessed 1 December 2023).